# 101

# BIBLE STORIES

# FOR ADULTS

## Faith, Purpose, and Renewal

Uncover the Hidden Layers of Scripture

Find Personal Meaning in Every Story & Live Out Biblical Truths

GRACEFUL GROWTH

# Contents

# A Note from the Author

Hi, I'm Monika, the heart and soul behind Graceful Growth and the author of 101 Bible Stories for Adults.

When I began working on 101 *Bible Stories for Adults*, my prayer was simple: to create a resource that helps everyday people connect with the timeless truths of Scripture in a way that feels clear, meaningful, and deeply personal.

Like many of you, I've experienced the overwhelming nature of life. The Bible, for me, has been more than just an ancient book; it's a living guide. Its stories speak into our struggles, its wisdom sheds light on our decisions, and its promises bring hope when we need it most.

This book was written with that in mind. Each story is designed to do more than retell events of the past. It's meant to draw you into God's presence, reveal His character, and show how His truth still transforms lives today.

Even though I publish under the name *Graceful Growth*, the voice and heart behind these pages are very real, and they're mine. This book is a culmination of my personal journey, and I'm excited to share it with you.

Thank you for inviting me into your spiritual journey. As you read, I hope that you'll find not just stories, but also encouragement, clarity, and a renewed sense of God's love for you. This book is here to support you in your spiritual growth.

With gratitude and faith,

—Monika

\*\*\*

**Let's stay connected!**
**Follow me on Facebook** for encouragement, behind-the-scenes updates, and early sneak peeks at new projects!

# READER BONUS

**BONUS # 1** - Start Strong with Your Free Prayer Journal

<< Scan the QR code to get your book >>

## BONUS # 2: Get Your Free Devotional for Couples

<< Scan here to download your book instantly >>

## Begin your 7-day journey of renewal now

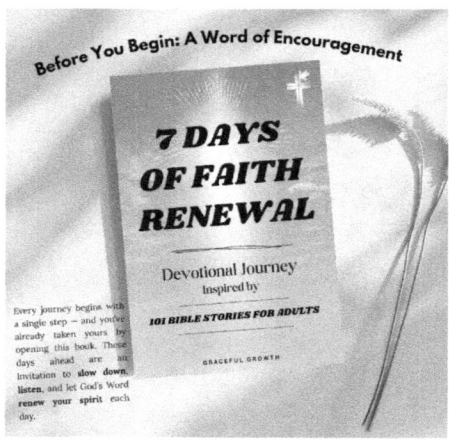

Simply scan the QR code to download your free devotional guide.

# Introduction

R ecently, I found myself at a spiritual crossroads, a place I believe many of you may have been. I yearned for a deeper connection with God, amidst the whirlwind of life, work, family, and endless responsibilities. My faith often felt like a distant shore I longed to reach but never quite did. I wanted to rediscover the wisdom of the Bible, yet its vastness usually left me feeling adrift.

It soon became clear that I wasn't the only one facing this struggle. Many adults, like you, share this desire for a stronger spiritual foundation but are unsure where to begin. The Bible, with its timeless wisdom, can sometimes feel overwhelming, its ancient texts difficult to relate to in our fast-paced world.

That's why I wrote *Bible Stories for Adults: Faith, Purpose, and Renewal.* This book is not just a collection of stories, but a guide, a compass in the vast sea of Scripture. It distills the most potent stories into reflections that fit naturally into the rhythms of daily life. Each one is a brief yet profound journey, offering a chance to engage with the heart of God's Word without the burden of lengthy study sessions.

Inside, you'll find a carefully chosen collection of stories—accounts that can inspire, challenge, and transform. These stories are not just for reading, but for experiencing personal growth and transformation. They are not presented simply as familiar retellings, but as invitations to reflect, to grow, and to see your own faith journey through a fresh and personal lens.

As you open these pages, I encourage you to come with both curiosity and openness. Be ready to uncover insights you may not have noticed before, to be stirred by the resilience of biblical figures, and to rediscover truths that remain as relevant today as when they were first spoken. This book is a journey, and your open mind is the key to unlocking its full potential.

So, are you ready to embark on this journey of faith, purpose, and renewal? Together, let's explore the richness of God's Word and discover how these stories can bring meaning, clarity, and encouragement to your life.

*Chapter 1*

# Foundations of Faith

G rowing up, I spent many Sunday mornings listening to the stories of Genesis. Back then, they felt like distant lessons, repeated but not always understood.

It wasn't until much later, sitting by a campfire on a crisp evening and watching the flames dance beneath a starry sky, that I began to see the deeper meaning.

We were talking about life, faith, and the struggles that come with both when someone asked:

**"Have you ever thought about the order in the chaos of creation?"**

That question stayed with me.

Suddenly, Genesis wasn't just about how the world began. It was about how God brings order to our lives, about finding peace in the middle of uncertainty.

This chapter explores those foundations of faith, not just as stories but as timeless truths that shape our daily lives

\*\*\*

# 1.1 Creation and Chaos: Lessons from Genesis

*Scripture Reference: Genesis 1:1–3:24*

The Bible opens with one of the most breathtaking statements in all of literature:

**"In the beginning God created the heavens and the earth." (Genesis 1:1, NIV)**

Genesis, the first book of the Bible, is both a beginning and a foundation. The word "Genesis" means "origins" or "beginnings." It sets the stage for everything that follows, not only in the biblical story but also in the story of humanity. For readers encountering this text for the first time, it helps to know that Genesis was written in a world filled with other creation accounts—many of which described violent battles between gods, where order came from conflict. Genesis presents something entirely different. God speaks, and order emerges. No struggle. No contest. His word brings forth a symphony of peace, structure, and life, a masterpiece of creation that inspires awe and reverence.

## The Days of Creation: A Story of Order

Genesis 1 describes creation as a carefully structured work, unfolding in stages:

**Day 1:** Light separates from darkness. Time itself begins.

**Day 2:** The sky stretches out, dividing the waters above from the waters below.

**Day 3:** Dry ground appears, and plants spring forth, covering the earth with life.

**Day 4:** The sun, moon, and stars mark days, seasons, and years, filling the heavens with light.

**Day 5:** The seas and skies teem with creatures—fish, birds, and all that fill the waters and air.

**Day 6:** God forms land animals, and finally, humanity is created in God's image, male and female, entrusted with care over all creation.

**Day 7:** God rests, not because He is weary, but to bless and set apart the Sabbath as a rhythm of life, a divine pattern of rest and renewal that we are called to emulate.

Each day builds upon the last, moving from chaos to order, from emptiness to abundance, from darkness to light. And with each stage, God declares it **"good."**

## Humanity's Role: Stewards, Not Owners

At the pinnacle of creation, God said:

*"Let us make mankind in our image... so that they may rule over... all the creatures that move along the ground."* **(Genesis 1:26, NIV)**

This calling is not about domination but stewardship. To be made in God's image is to reflect His character by caring for the earth, honoring relationships, and living with intentionality. Being made in God's image means we share in His creativity, His love, His justice, and His care for His creation. From the very beginning, humanity's role was not to exploit creation but to cultivate it, to mirror God's care and responsibility in our own lives.

How we treat the environment matters.

How we treat one another matters.

How we use our time, talents, and resources matters.

God's design calls us to reflect His intentionality in the way we live, love, and lead. It's not just about existing, but about living with purpose, care, and love.

## The Entrance of Chaos: A Foreshadowing

Genesis also gives us a glimpse of the fragility of this harmony. Humanity was free to enjoy the fullness of creation, yet freedom included the possibility of disobedience. A boundary was set in Eden, and with it came a choice. Though the garden was filled with abundance, the seeds of temptation would one day test Adam and Eve's trust in God.

## Prayer Prompt: Stewardship in Action

Ask God to show you how to be a faithful steward of what He has entrusted to you, whether that is the environment, your relationships, your time, or your talents. Pray for wisdom to act with care and integrity, and for a heart that reflects His love, even in small, everyday actions such as showing kindness to a stranger, forgiving someone who has wronged you, using your talents to help others, or making sustainable choices in your daily life.

---

### Community Reflection (For those reading in groups)

- In what ways do we see God restoring order in our families, churches, or neighborhoods?

- In a world of consumerism and rapid change, how can we reflect His vision of stewardship with courage and grace?

- How can we encourage one another to see stewardship not just as responsibility, but as worship and gratitude to God?

---

## Final Reflections: God's Design and Our Calling

The opening chapters of Genesis remind us that God brings order out of chaos, light out of darkness, and purpose out of emptiness. They affirm that we are created in His image and entrusted with His creation. Even when our choices introduce disorder, God's redemptive hand is already at work. This means that God is constantly working to bring good out of our mistakes, to restore what is broken, and to bring us back into right relationship with Him. The story of creation is not only about the beginning of the world—it is about the beginning of our story with God, a story that continues even now.

## 1.2 The Fall: Humanity's First Choice and Its Consequences

*Scripture Reference: Genesis 3:1–24*

After the beauty of creation and the harmony of Eden, Genesis takes a sobering turn. Paradise was not only a gift, it was also a test of trust. Humanity was given freedom, and with freedom came the possibility of choice. This choice would alter the course of history and the nature of our relationship with God.

### The First Temptation

One day, a serpent approached Eve with words meant to twist God's truth and plant doubt.

**"Did God really say, 'You must not eat from any tree in the garden'?" (Genesis 3:1, NIV)**

It was a distortion of God's command, designed to make obedience sound restrictive instead of protective. Eve looked at the tree again. The fruit seemed good, desirable for wisdom, and attractive to the eye. She reached out, took it, and ate. Then she gave some to Adam, who was with her, and he ate also (Genesis 3:6, NIV).

In that moment, everything shifted. Innocence gave way to shame. Peace was replaced with fear. Adam and Eve, once unashamed in God's presence, now hid among the trees of the garden.

### The Ripple Effects of Disobedience

The Fall was not just a single act of disobedience; it was a rupture in humanity's relationship with God. Its consequences rippled outward, shaping the world that followed.

Humanity's intimacy with God was broken, replaced by distance and alienation. The natural world, once abundant and harmonious, became marked by toil, decay, and pain. Human relationships, once whole, became tangled with blame, conflict, and power struggles.

Sin entered, and its shadow stretched across every generation.

Yet even in this moment of judgment, mercy was still present.

*"The Lord God made garments of skin for Adam and his wife and clothed them."* (Genesis 3:21, NIV)

This tender act of covering was more than practical. It was a profound expression of God's mercy, foreshadowing His greater plan of redemption, when He would one day provide a covering through Christ.

## The Fall and Our Own Choices

Adam and Eve's story is not just history. It mirrors our own lives. We, too, are tempted to question God's goodness and to believe the promise that life outside His design, which is a life of obedience and trust, will be more fulfilling. Like them, our choices affect not only ourselves but also the lives of others around us.

When we stumble, we face the same decision Adam and Eve faced: Will we hide in shame, or will we return to God for forgiveness and restoration? The Fall reminds us that while sin creates separation, God's grace always makes a way back.

## Prayer Prompt: Choices and Consequences

Bring before God a recent decision, such as a moral dilemma at work or a personal relationship issue, that tested your values or integrity. Ask Him for wisdom to learn from it, grace to move forward, and strength to make choices that bring restoration and peace. Even when we stumble, His redemption is already at work.

## Community Reflection

- What doubts or temptations feel most present in our world today?

- How can we support one another in making choices that honor God, even when culture pulls us in the opposite direction?

- In what ways can remembering God's original design for humanity help us resist the lies of temptation today?

## Final Reflections: The Foundations of Our Faith

From creation to the Fall, Genesis lays the foundation for understanding our world, our purpose, and our need for God. He brings order from chaos and entrusts us with His creation. Our choices matter, carrying real consequences—but His mercy is greater than our failure.

As we reflect on these truths, may we learn to seek the order God is bringing into our lives, live faithfully as caretakers of His gifts, and lean into His grace when we fall short. The story of the Fall is not just about brokenness—it is also about hope, because even when humanity turned away, God never walked away, always offering a path back to Him.

\*\*\*

## 1.3 Noah's Ark: Faith in the Midst of Uncertainty

*Scripture Reference: Genesis 5:32–10:1*

The story of Noah begins in a world consumed by corruption and violence. Humanity, created for fellowship with God and stewardship of the earth, had turned away from both.

Scripture tells us that **"the Lord saw how great the wickedness of the human race had become on the earth, and that every inclination of the thoughts of the human heart was only evil all the time"** (Genesis 6:5, NIV).

In the midst of this brokenness, one man stood out.

Noah was described as **"a righteous man, blameless among the people of his time, and he walked faithfully with God"** (Genesis 6:9, NIV). While the world around him spiraled deeper into chaos, Noah's life reflected a different path. He lived with integrity. He listened for God's voice. He resisted the tide of corruption that swept through his generation.

Then came a command unlike any other: **"Build an ark."**

## Faith to Obey the Unthinkable

Imagine the skepticism Noah must have faced. An ark large enough to hold his family, pairs of animals, and provisions for an unknown future? At a time when the concept of a global flood seemed absurd, his obedience looked like foolishness to those around him. The neighbors must have whispered. Some likely mocked openly.

Yet Noah persisted.

Day after day, plank by plank, he followed God's instructions in faith (Genesis 6:13–22, NIV). What others dismissed as folly was, in reality, preparation for salvation. When the floodwaters finally rose, Noah's trust was vindicated.

## The Flood: A Story of Judgment and Renewal

The flood was more than a disaster. It was a divine act of judgment against pervasive evil, but it was also a story of mercy. God preserved a remnant through Noah and his family, ensuring that creation would not end in destruction.

When the waters subsided, Noah stepped onto dry ground and built an altar to the Lord. In response, God made a covenant not only with Noah but with all of creation: **"Never again will the waters become a flood to destroy all life"** (Genesis 9:15, NIV).

The rainbow, stretched across the sky, became the sign of this promise. It was not simply a mark of protection, but a reminder of God's enduring commitment to renewal and relationship.

Ancient cultures also told flood stories, such as the Epic of Gilgamesh. Yet in those accounts, survival was often arbitrary, determined by capricious gods. Genesis presents a radically different picture: a God who judges with purpose, who saves through grace, and who binds Himself to humanity through covenant.

## Noah's Faith in Our Own Lives

Noah's story is more than ancient history. It echoes in our own journeys of faith.

We, too, are sometimes called to trust God when His plans seem beyond reason. Building an "ark" today may look like stepping into a vocation, a calling, or an act of obedience that others cannot understand. It may mean standing for truth in a culture that scoffs at faith. It may mean persevering in prayer or service when results are not yet visible.

And like the rainbow, we are given reminders of God's faithfulness. They may come in answered prayers, in moments of unexpected provision, or in the quiet assurance of His presence during difficult seasons. These are not mere coincidences, but signs of His enduring faithfulness, His promises that sustain us when circumstances feel overwhelming.

## Prayer Prompt: Building Your Own Ark

Ask God for the faith to trust His plans, even when they defy logic or invite ridicule. Pray for the perseverance to walk in obedience day by day and for the eyes to notice the "rainbows" He places in your life as signs of His enduring faithfulness.

---

**Community Reflection**

- What might "building an ark" look like in today's world—standing firm in faith even when it seems countercultural?

- How do God's promises sustain us when circumstances feel overwhelming?

- What small daily acts of obedience can we practice that prepare us to trust God in bigger challenges?

---

**Final Reflections: Trusting in the Promise**

Noah's story shows us that faith is not always about understanding—it is about trusting. The flood reminds us of God's justice and His mercy. The rainbow assures us that His promises endure.

When we face seasons of uncertainty, may we, like Noah, have the courage to obey, the strength to endure, and the hope to see God's covenant faithfulness written across our skies.

***

# 1.4 The Tower of Babel: Ambition vs. Divine Will

*Scripture Reference: Genesis 11:1–9*

After the flood, humanity began to multiply again, spreading across the land with renewed hope. Families grew, villages turned into towns, and the earth started to feel alive once more. What made this period unique was that everyone spoke the same language. There were no misunderstandings, no barriers between tribes, no cultural walls dividing people. Unity and cooperation were at their peak.

In this atmosphere of shared purpose, an idea was born. With hearts filled not with gratitude toward God but with ambition for themselves, the people dreamed of building something monumental. They said:

**"Come, let us build ourselves a city, with a tower that reaches to the heavens, so that we may make a name for ourselves; otherwise we will be scattered over the face of the whole earth." (Genesis 11:4, NIV)**

It was more than an architectural dream. It was a declaration of independence. By constructing this tower, they sought permanence, security, and glory on their own terms. The project symbolized humanity's desire to control their future, to exalt themselves above their Creator, to leave behind a legacy untouchable by God.

For a time, the construction must have been impressive—stone upon stone rising higher, the people united in a common cause. But beneath the teamwork and progress lay pride, fear, and rebellion.

## God's Intervention

God saw their hearts. He recognized that this unity, left unchecked, would lead not to flourishing but to arrogance and destruction. In His wisdom, He stepped in—not with fire or flood, but with language. He confused their speech so they could no longer understand one another. Work came to a halt.

Misunderstandings multiplied. Frustration spread. And soon, the people scattered across the earth, abandoning the great tower that stood unfinished as a monument to human limitation. (Genesis 11:7–9, NIV)

## Babel: A Lesson in Humility and Diversity

Babel reminds us that God was not punishing human creativity or progress. He was protecting a purpose. By scattering the nations, He shifted the focus away from human-centered glory to God-centered mission.

In the ancient Near East, stepped temple structures called ziggurats were built as gateways between heaven and earth. These were massive, pyramid-like structures with a series of terraces or platforms, each smaller than the one below it, and a temple at the top. The tower at Babel likely echoed this practice. Still, Genesis makes a radical claim: no matter how high humanity builds, true transcendence belongs to God alone.

The lesson is clear: greatness is not in the monuments we construct but in the God we serve. Unity is not found in forced conformity but in the harmony of diversity shaped by His design.

## The Babel Narrative Today

Our modern world is also marked by ambition, success, and the pursuit of legacy. Yet the story of Babel asks hard questions:

Are we building for God's glory or our own?

Do we value diversity as God's gift, or do we try to mold everyone into sameness?

How do we balance innovation and progress with humility and dependence on God?

The unfinished tower continues to speak. It warns us against self-exaltation but also invites us to surrender our ambitions and align them with God's greater plan, which is the overarching purpose and design that God has for each of us, as revealed in His Word and through His guidance.

## Prayer Prompt: Surrendering Ambition to God

Ask God to align your ambitions with His purpose. Pray for humility, wisdom, and a heart that seeks unity through His design rather than self-driven effort.

## Community Reflection

- What kinds of "towers" do we see in our world today—projects or pursuits driven more by pride than purpose?

- How can we practice humility in our careers, relationships, or ministries while still striving for excellence?

- In what ways can our communities shift from building for our own name to building for God's glory?

## Final Reflections: True Greatness Redefined

The Tower of Babel reminds us that ambition without God leads to scattering and confusion, but walking with Him leads to harmony and purpose. Greatness is not measured in monuments but in obedience, humility, and unity rooted in His design.

$$***$$

# 1.5 Abraham's Call: A Journey of Faith and Obedience

*Scripture Reference: Genesis 12:1–22:19*

Abraham's call was one of those moments that changed everything.

Imagine living a comfortable life in **Ur**, one of the most advanced cities of the ancient world. Located in Mesopotamia (modern-day Iraq), Ur was wealthy, bustling with trade, and filled with grand temples dedicated to the moon god. Life there promised security, prosperity, and stability. For Abraham and his family, it would have been the center of opportunity and culture.

And yet, in the midst of this thriving city, God spoke to him with a call that defied logic:

**"Go from your country, your people, and your father's household to the land I will show you."** (Genesis 12:1, NIV)

No roadmap. No details. Just a promise.

A promise of land.

A promise of descendants.

A promise of blessing that would extend to all nations.

Abraham, despite his age and Sarah's barrenness, dared to embark on this seemingly impossible journey. His determination to trust in God's promise, even when it seemed illogical, is truly inspiring.

## Faith Without Seeing

Abraham's journey was anything but smooth. He faced famine upon entering Canaan (Genesis 12:10, NIV). He made mistakes, sometimes wavering in fear—such as when he misled others about Sarah being his sister (Genesis 12:11–13, NIV). He waited decades for the son God had promised, at times wondering if the promise would ever come (Genesis 17:17–18, NIV).

And yet, he clung to God's word.

**"Against all hope, Abraham in hope believed and so became the father of many nations."** (Romans 4:18, NIV)

Abraham's faith, though not perfect, was persistent. He continued to walk, continued to trust, even when the evidence seemed to say otherwise. This persistence in faith is a source of encouragement for us all.

The ultimate test came years later, when God asked him to sacrifice Isaac—the very son of promise (Genesis 22:1-2, NIV). Standing on Mount Moriah, torn between obedience and love, Abraham uttered a statement of profound trust:

**"God himself will provide the lamb."** (Genesis 22:8, NIV)

And God did, providing a ram in Isaac's place (Genesis 22:13, NIV). This moment revealed that Abraham's faith wasn't just personal. It set the tone for generations. His trust became the model of covenant faith, showing that God's promises are sure even when the path is unclear.

## What Abraham Teaches Us About Faith

Abraham's story reminds us that faith is not passive. It is active, lived out in decisions, trust, and obedience. His faith required leaving behind comfort to embrace uncertainty. It meant waiting on promises that seemed delayed beyond reason. It meant obedience that defied logic.

And yet, his faith was not flawless. He stumbled, doubted, and sometimes tried to take matters into his own hands. Still, God remained faithful, proving that even imperfect faith can be the soil where His promises grow. Abraham's journey shows us that faith is not about never failing, but about returning to trust again and again, knowing God's word is sure.

Where is God calling you to step out in faith?

Are you clinging to security instead of stepping into the unknown?

How can you hold onto God's promises, even when they seem delayed?

## Prayer Prompt: Walking in Faith

Ask God to give you the courage to follow His calling, even when the path is unclear. Pray for patience in waiting, trust in His timing, and strength to persevere when faith feels costly.

---

**Community Reflection**

- What "comfort zones" might God be asking us to leave behind to grow in faith?

- How can we encourage one another during seasons of waiting or uncertainty?

- What does trusting God's promises look like in practical, everyday decisions?

---

## Final Reflections: The Foundations of Faith

From Noah's unwavering obedience to Abraham's trust in unseen promises, these stories remind us that faith is not always logical, but it is always worth it. God calls us to build, trust, and follow, even when we don't have the whole picture. His promises never fail, even when they take time to unfold.

As we reflect on these foundational stories, may we have the faith to build our "arks" even when others doubt, surrender our ambitions to God's greater plan, and trust His promises even when they seem impossible. Because faith is not about certainty—it is about trust in the One who is always faithful.

✴✴✴

## 1.6 Sodom and Gomorrah: Morality and Divine Justice

### Scripture Reference: Genesis 18:16–19:29

Sodom and Gomorrah were cities of prosperity in the fertile plain near the Jordan River. To the outside observer, they seemed like centers of abundance and opportunity (Genesis 13:10–13, NIV). But beneath their wealth and busyness lay a troubling reality—a society marked by arrogance, cruelty, and corruption. Scripture describes their sins as "grievous" and their wickedness as so severe that the outcry against them reached heaven (Genesis 18:20–21, NIV).

The cries of the oppressed rose to God, and He responded. This was not an arbitrary judgment but a reckoning—a moment when divine justice confronted unchecked evil. Yet before destruction came, something extraordinary happened: God invited Abraham into a conversation about mercy.

## A Conversation with God: Abraham's Plea for Mercy

Before judgment came, Scripture pauses on one of the most astonishing dialogues in the Bible: Abraham standing before God and pleading for mercy.

**"Will you sweep away the righteous with the wicked?"** (Genesis 18:23, NIV)

With humility and courage, Abraham began a negotiation unlike any other. First fifty. Then forty-five. Then forty. Thirty. Twenty. Finally ten. With each request, Abraham pressed further into God's heart. With each reply, God agreed: if even a small remnant of righteousness remained, the cities would be spared (Genesis 18:24–32, NIV).

This moment teaches us more than just persistence. It reveals the character of God—patient, willing to listen, slow to anger, and abounding in mercy. It also shows us something profound about the role of God's people:

**Intercession is powerful.** Abraham dared to plead not only for his family but for entire cities. His boldness reminds us that our prayers can impact lives beyond our own.

**Righteousness matters.** Even a small remnant could have preserved Sodom and Gomorrah. Holiness is never wasted—it protects and blesses far more than we see.

**Mercy tempers judgment.** God does not delight in destruction. His willingness to relent shows that His justice always carries the possibility of grace.

For Abraham, this exchange was an act of faith and compassion. For us, it is a model of advocacy. In our time, standing "in the gap" means interceding for communities in crisis, praying for those far from God, and speaking up for the voiceless when injustice prevails.

## The Destruction: Judgment and Redemption

Despite Abraham's plea, not even ten righteous people could be found within the city walls. The wickedness of Sodom and Gomorrah had become pervasive, and the cries of injustice could no longer be ignored.

Two angels entered the city and were welcomed by Lot, Abraham's nephew. But by nightfall, the men of Sodom surrounded the house, demanding that Lot hand over his guests so they could abuse them (Genesis 19:4–5, NIV). Lot, in a courageous act of righteousness, refused to hand over his guests, even at the risk of his own safety. It was a horrifying picture of depravity and hostility toward the very hospitality God had commanded His people to uphold.

At dawn, after urging Lot and his family to flee, the judgment fell:

**"Then the Lord rained down burning sulfur on Sodom and Gomorrah—from the Lord out of the heavens."** (Genesis 19:24, NIV)

Flames engulfed the cities. The lush valley, once compared to the garden of the Lord (Genesis 13:10, NIV), became a desolate wasteland. Fertility gave way to barrenness. Prosperity turned to ruin. It was not only a destruction of buildings but of a culture that had persistently rejected righteousness and oppressed the vulnerable.

Yet even in judgment, mercy broke through. God spared Lot and his daughters, physically pulling them from danger when hesitation nearly cost them their lives (Genesis 19:15–16, NIV). His wife, however, looked back longingly and was consumed, turned into a pillar of salt (Genesis 19:26, NIV). Her fate stands as a sobering reminder of the danger of clinging to the past when God calls us forward.

The destruction of Sodom and Gomorrah became a lasting symbol. Later prophets and writers used it as a warning that unchecked wickedness leads to ruin (Isaiah 1:9–10; Jude 1:7, NIV). To the original audience, it reinforced a simple truth: no city, no culture, no empire is above God's call to justice and holiness.

This moment reminds us that:

Mercy is extended to those willing to receive it with trust.

Even in the darkest moments, God provides a way out.

Looking backward can keep us from stepping into God's salvation.

## A Warning and a Call to Action

The story of Sodom and Gomorrah is not only about destruction—it is also a call to justice, mercy, and advocacy. Scripture echoes this call throughout:

**"Learn to do right; seek justice. Defend the oppressed."** (Isaiah 1:17, NIV)

We are reminded to:

Recognize injustice in our world and refuse to ignore it.

Advocate for others, interceding as Abraham did.

Choose righteousness daily, knowing that our choices shape both our lives and our communities.

## Prayer Prompt: Seeking Justice and Mercy

Ask God to open your eyes to the injustices around you and give you the courage to stand for truth and righteousness. Pray for mercy where there is brokenness and for wisdom to be a voice of change in your family, workplace, and community. Remember, prayer is not just a passive act of petition, but a powerful tool for advocating for justice and mercy in our world.

Because true faith isn't just about avoiding judgment—it's about living as a reflection of God's justice, mercy, and love.

**Community Reflection**

- What does it look like to "stand in the gap" for others in today's world?

- How can we practice both truth and mercy when addressing injustice in our families, workplaces, or communities?

- In what ways can prayer and intercession shape the way we respond to the brokenness around us?

## Final Reflections: A God of Justice and Mercy

Sodom and Gomorrah's destruction is a sobering reminder that injustice cannot be ignored. Yet the story also reveals a God who listens to intercession, shows mercy to those willing to follow Him, and calls His people to live differently.

May we be people who do not turn a blind eye to suffering but instead advocate for justice, live righteously, and cling to God's mercy. For even in judgment, His love is still at work, pointing us toward redemption. Let us remember that our daily choices to live righteously and advocate for justice can make a significant difference in our communities and the world.

# Chapter 2

# Patriarchs and Promises

I grew up hearing about Abraham and Isaac, their names familiar yet distant, their stories known but not fully understood.

But one day, I sat alone in a quiet room, sunlight streaming in, lost in thought. It was in that stillness that I finally grasped the weight of faith and sacrifice—how much trust it takes to walk a path without knowing where it leads.

This chapter explores moments of divine encounters and unwavering trust, stories of people who dared to believe in promises unseen.

***

## 2.1 Isaac's Sacrifice: Trust Beyond Understanding

Scripture Reference: Genesis 22:1–19

The story of Abraham and Isaac, one of the most profound and challenging narratives in the entire Bible, resonates through centuries as a testament to faith, obedience, and divine provision. To the original audience, this account would have carried enormous weight, not only because it involved the patriarch Abraham, but also because it revealed the very character of God.

Imagine the scene. Abraham, who had waited decades for a promised son, finally held Isaac—the child through whom God's covenant was meant to continue (Genesis 17:19, NIV). Isaac was not just a beloved child; he was the living reminder of God's faithfulness. And then came the unthinkable command:

**"Take your son, your only son, whom you love—Isaac—and go to the region of Moriah. Sacrifice him there as a burnt offering on a mountain I will show you."** (Genesis 22:2, NIV)

The words must have pierced Abraham's heart. In the surrounding cultures of the ancient Near East, child sacrifice was tragically practiced as a way to appease the gods. But Abraham's God was different. This command was not about cruelty. It was about testing faith and revealing that true devotion rests in trust, not ritual death.

## Faith at the Altar

Abraham rose early the next morning, setting out with Isaac toward Mount Moriah. Every step of the journey must have been heavy, filled with silence and unspoken anguish. The weight of the command, the love for his son, and the trust in God must have been a tumultuous storm in Abraham's heart (Genesis 22:3–4, NIV). When Isaac asked, **"Where is the lamb for the burnt offering?"** Abraham answered with words of trust that would echo through generations:

**"God himself will provide the lamb for the burnt offering, my son."** (Genesis 22:8, NIV)

At the altar, Abraham bound Isaac and raised the knife. Then came the moment of divine intervention:

**"Do not lay a hand on the boy... Now I know that you fear God, because you have not withheld from me your son, your only son."** (Genesis 22:12, NIV).

This divine intervention, a clear sign of God's presence, was a moment of reassurance for Abraham.

And there, caught in a thicket, was a ram. God had provided a substitute (Genesis 22:13, NIV). Imagine the relief and joy that must have flooded Abraham and Isaac's hearts at that moment. Their faith had been tested, and they had emerged victorious, experiencing the reward of unwavering trust in God.

## What Isaac's Sacrifice Teaches Us

This moment was more than a test of obedience. It was a revelation of God's faithfulness.

God provided in the most impossible moment.

His promises did not fail, even when they seemed on the brink of loss.

Faith requires surrender when logic and reason cannot explain the path ahead.

Isaac's quiet obedience is also remarkable. He was strong enough to resist, yet Scripture records no protest. His trust mirrored Abraham's, showing that faith often requires not only action but also stillness and surrender, bringing a sense of peace that comes with confidence in God.

## Our Mount Moriah Moments

We, too, face times when God calls us into the unknown, asking for trust when the outcome seems unbearable or unclear. Like Abraham and Isaac, we are invited to walk in faith, believing that God provides even when circumstances look impossible.

What is your Mount Moriah?

Where is God asking you to release control?

Are you willing to trust His provision when the cost feels too high?

## Prayer Prompt: Trust in the Unknown

Bring before God a situation in your life that requires trust beyond your understanding. Ask Him for peace in the waiting, strength in the surrender, and the faith to believe that His provision is already at work.

**Community Reflection**

- How does Abraham's obedience challenge the way we think about trust?

- What does Isaac's quiet surrender reveal about faith under pressure?

- How can we encourage one another to keep trusting when the outcome is unclear?

## Final Reflections: God Provides

The story of Abraham and Isaac is not about a God who demands what we cannot give—it is about a God who provides what we cannot imagine. Centuries later, this story would foreshadow another sacrifice, when God did not spare His own Son but gave Him up for us all (Romans 8:32, NIV).

When we face our own Mount Moriah moments, may we walk in faith, surrender our fears, and trust that God will always provide.

***

## 2.2 Jacob's Ladder: Dreams and Divine Encounters

Scripture Reference: Genesis 28:10–22

Jacob's life was at a turning point. He was not a man of peace at this moment; he was a fugitive. Having deceived his father and stolen his brother Esau's blessing (Genesis 27:35–36, NIV), Jacob fled from home, weighed down by guilt and fear. Alone on the journey to his uncle Laban's house in Haran, he carried no royal caravan or mighty protection, only the weight of his choices and an uncertain future.

Exhausted, Jacob stopped for the night in a desolate place. With only a stone for a pillow, he lay down under the stars, the cold earth beneath him. To human eyes, this looked like rock bottom, yet it became the setting for one of Scripture's most extraordinary encounters.

**"He had a dream in which he saw a stairway resting on the earth, with its top reaching to heaven, and the angels of God were ascending and descending on it."** (Genesis 28:12, NIV)

This was no ordinary dream. The stairway, sometimes translated as "ladder," was a divine revelation, a connection between heaven and earth. The God of his fathers had not abandoned him. Even in flight, Jacob discovered that God was nearer than he ever imagined.

## A Divine Promise in an Unexpected Place

In the dream, God Himself spoke, reaffirming the covenant made with Abraham and Isaac:

**"I am with you and will watch over you wherever you go, and I will bring you back to this land. I will not leave you until I have done what I have promised you."** (Genesis 28:15, NIV)

When Jacob awoke, he was overcome with awe. He declared:

*"Surely the Lord is in this place, and I was not aware of it."* (Genesis 28:16, NIV)

What Jacob thought was an ordinary wilderness had become holy ground. In response, he set up the stone he had slept on as a pillar, anointing it with oil as a sacred marker, naming the place Bethel—**"house of God"** (Genesis 28:18–19, NIV).

As already mentioned, in the ancient Near East, temple towers known as ziggurats were often built to reach toward the heavens. Jacob's dream, however, reversed the imagery. Instead of humanity striving to climb up to the divine, it was God who reached down, showing Jacob that His presence was not dependent on human effort but on divine grace.

## What Jacob's Ladder Teaches Us

Jacob's story is more than a dream; it is a reminder that God meets us in the most unexpected places, even in the middle of our mistakes and uncertainty.

God speaks in unlikely circumstances, even when we feel far from Him.

Divine encounters can happen anywhere if our hearts are open to see them.

Grace meets us even when we are running from our past.

Jacob marked his encounter with a stone, not to worship the place, but to remember the presence of God who had met him there. In the same way, we are called to "mark" the moments when God meets us—those sacred encounters that remind us He is always near.

## Recognizing Our Own Sacred Encounters

We may not dream of ladders filled with angels, but we all experience moments of divine nearness.

A conversation that changes our perspective.

An answered prayer that arrives at just the right time.

A deep peace that steadies us in chaos.

These are our modern Bethels, the sacred markers reminding us that God is with us, even when we were unaware.

## Prayer Prompt: Remembering God's Presence

Reflect on a time when you experienced God's presence unexpectedly—in prayer, in crisis, or in stillness. Thank Him for that moment and ask for eyes to recognize His nearness in your daily life, even in ordinary settings.

---

**Community Reflection**

- How does Jacob's encounter encourage us when we feel far from God?

- What practices help us "mark" God's presence in our lives so we do not forget His faithfulness?

- How can we remind one another in community that God often meets us in unexpected places, just as He did with Jacob?

---

## Final Reflections: Walking in Trust and Awareness

From Abraham's sacrifice to Jacob's dream, these stories remind us that faith is not only about promises to be fulfilled in the future. It is also about God's presence in the present. Faith requires trust even when the path is uncertain. God provides in impossible moments. Divine encounters surround us if we are willing to see them.

As we walk forward, may we trust that God is always near, mark the moments of His faithfulness, and live with the confidence that even in our wilderness we are never alone.

**\*\*\***

## 2.3 Joseph's Resilience: From Pit to Palace

Scripture Reference: Genesis 37:1–50:26

Imagine a young boy walking through the fields of Canaan, his multicolored coat glinting in the sunlight, a gift from his father that spoke of special favor. Joseph carried not only this robe but also dreams—visions of greatness where his brothers bowed before him

(Genesis 37:5-7, NIV). To Joseph, these dreams were glimpses of God's plan. To his brothers, they were salt in a wound already raw with jealousy.

As he approached them that day, perhaps eager to share news or to be near them, their hearts burned with resentment. Before Joseph could grasp what was happening, rough hands seized him. His robe, the very symbol of his father's love, was stripped away. He was thrown into a pit, listening to their voices above as they debated his fate (Genesis 37:23-24, NIV).

That pit was the beginning of a long and unexpected journey. A betrayal so deep it tore him from home, sending him into a future he could never have imagined.

Yet Joseph's story was not one of defeat. It became a story of resilience, of a faith that bent under pressure but did not break.

## From Servitude to Prison

Sold to traders and carried into Egypt, Joseph's life as a free son ended, and his life as an enslaved person began. In the house of Potiphar, an Egyptian official, Joseph faced the challenge of rebuilding from nothing. Yet even in this foreign land, far from his father and homeland, Joseph's life bore fruit.

**"The Lord was with Joseph so that he prospered, and he lived in the house of his Egyptian master."** (Genesis 39:2, NIV)

He rose in rank and was entrusted with responsibility. But just as stability seemed within reach, betrayal came again. Wrongly accused by Potiphar's wife, Joseph was thrown into prison (Genesis 39:20, NIV).

It would have been easy to give in to bitterness. To believe that faith had failed. But Joseph did not surrender to despair.

## Faith in the Midst of Injustice

In prison, Joseph remained faithful. He served. He listened. He interpreted dreams for fellow prisoners, always pointing to God as the source of his insight (Genesis 40:8, NIV). Even there, God's presence did not leave him:

**"The Lord was with him; he showed him kindness and granted him favor in the eyes of the prison warden."** (Genesis 39:21, NIV)

Years passed in waiting, years where hope might have dimmed. Then came a turning point. Pharaoh himself had a troubling dream—seven fat cows devoured by seven gaunt ones, seven healthy heads of grain swallowed by withered stalks (Genesis 41:1–7, NIV). Egypt's wise men were baffled. Joseph was summoned.

Standing before the most powerful ruler of his day, Joseph spoke words of humility:

**"I cannot do it, but God will give Pharaoh the answer he desires."** (Genesis 41:16, NIV)

Through divine wisdom, Joseph explained the dream: seven years of abundance would be followed by seven years of famine (Genesis 41:29–30, NIV). His counsel to prepare impressed Pharaoh, who placed Joseph second only to himself in command of Egypt (Genesis 41:39–41, NIV).

From prisoner to ruler. From pit to palace. Joseph's rise was not luck, but providence. God was weaving redemption into every setback.

## Joseph's Resilience and Our Own Trials

Joseph's journey reminds us that what looks like defeat may be the groundwork for future blessing. His life shows us that:

Betrayal does not cancel God's purpose.

Waiting does not mean abandonment.

Injustice does not silence God's presence.

Like Joseph, we too face pits of betrayal, seasons of waiting, and moments of false accusation. The question is whether we will let those moments define us, or whether we will trust God to use them as preparation for something greater. And in these moments, the support and encouragement of our Christian community can be a powerful source of strength and resilience.

## Prayer Prompt: Finding Purpose in Hardship

Ask God to help you see purpose in the trials you face. Pray for resilience to endure, for faith to remain steadfast, and for wisdom to recognize how He is shaping you through hardship into someone ready for greater things.

---

### Community Reflection

- How does Joseph's perseverance challenge us when we face setbacks?

- What role does forgiveness play in resilience, especially when others betray us?

- How can we encourage one another to keep faith alive during long seasons of waiting?

---

## Final Reflections: Providence in Every Season

Joseph's life reveals that God's providence is often most visible in hindsight. From the pit to the palace, from betrayal to reconciliation, God was at work. Take a moment to reflect on your own life and consider the times when God's providence was at work, even in the midst of trials.

Our trials may not make sense in the moment, but faith allows us to trust that God is writing a bigger story. May we, like Joseph, endure with resilience, cling to His promises, and believe that even the most complicated steps can lead us closer to His greater purpose.

## 2.4 The Forgiveness of Joseph: Healing Family Wounds

Scripture Reference: Genesis 42:1–45:28; 50:15–21

Years passed, and Joseph's life looked nothing like the frightened boy once thrown into a pit. He had risen to power in Egypt, second only to Pharaoh himself, surrounded by wealth, influence, and honor. From the outside, he had everything a person could dream of. Yet even in the heights of authority, the memory of betrayal lingered—until one day, the past walked unexpectedly into the room.

The famine that swept across the land had driven people from distant regions to Egypt in search of food. Among them were Joseph's own brothers—the very ones who had plotted against him, who had ripped away his coat of many colors, and who had sold him into slavery. They bowed low before him, unaware of who he was (Genesis 42:6, NIV). In that moment, Joseph's dreams of long ago were fulfilled before his eyes. But how would he respond?

### A Test of the Heart

Joseph had every reason to seek revenge. He could have used his power to repay their cruelty with judgment. Yet instead of acting rashly, he chose to test their hearts.

He accused them of being spies (Genesis 42:9, NIV). He demanded that they bring their youngest brother, Benjamin, to Egypt. He secretly placed a silver cup in Benjamin's sack, creating a scenario that would force them to reveal their true character (Genesis 44:1–12, NIV).

Would they abandon Benjamin as they had abandoned him? Or had they changed?

When Joseph saw their genuine grief and willingness to protect their younger brother, his heart broke open. He could no longer contain his emotions.

**"Joseph said to his brothers, 'I am Joseph! Is my father still living?' But his brothers were not able to answer him, because they were terrified at his presence."** (Genesis 45:3, NIV)

In their shock and fear, they waited for punishment. Instead, Joseph offered something entirely unexpected. He forgave.

## Forgiveness as a Choice, Not a Feeling

In Joseph's time, revenge was not only expected but seen as just. Forgiveness was rare, unthinkable, even shameful. Yet Joseph chose a different way. His words revealed a man who saw beyond human motives to God's greater plan:

**"You intended to harm me, but God intended it for good to accomplish what is now being done, the saving of many lives."** (Genesis 50:20, NIV)

Joseph's forgiveness did not dismiss the pain of betrayal. It did not erase the memories of the pit, the slavery, or the prison. But it transformed his story from one of bitterness to one of redemption. By choosing forgiveness, Joseph broke the cycle of revenge that had defined his family for generations. He restored his brothers, reunited with his father, and ensured the survival of his people.

Forgiveness did not erase the past—but it healed the future.

## What Joseph's Forgiveness Teaches Us

Joseph's story reminds us that we all carry wounds from the past. Betrayal, rejection, or broken relationships can weigh heavily on our hearts. Forgiveness is not always easy, nor is it always immediate. It is not forgetting—it is choosing to release bitterness and allow God's grace to transform pain into healing.

When Joseph forgave, he gave his brothers peace, but he also gave himself freedom. The same is true for us. Forgiveness may not change the past, but it changes the future.

## Prayer Prompt: The Power to Forgive

Bring before God a relationship where forgiveness feels difficult. Ask Him for the courage to release resentment and for the strength to take steps toward reconciliation. Pray for a heart softened by grace, one that chooses peace over bitterness.

Forgiveness is not about excusing what was wrong. It is about moving forward in the power of grace.

---

## Community Reflection

- How does Joseph's choice to forgive challenge the way we think about justice and revenge?

- What relationships in our families or communities might need the healing power of forgiveness?

- How can we support one another in the slow, sometimes painful process of reconciliation?

---

## Final Reflections: Resilience and Reconciliation

Joseph's story is one of suffering and triumph. Still, more deeply, it is a testimony of trust, resilience, and the power of forgiveness.

He endured betrayal but held fast to his faith.

He faced injustice but chose healing.

He recognized that God's providence could redeem even the darkest wrongs.

As we reflect on Joseph's journey, may we persevere in our own seasons of difficulty, choose forgiveness instead of resentment, and believe that what others mean for harm, God can turn into good. Because forgiveness is not weakness—it is one of the most extraordinary acts of strength, and it opens the door to reconciliation and peace.

***

## 2.5 Moses and the Burning Bush: A Call to Leadership

Scripture Reference: Exodus 3:1–4:17

It was just another ordinary day in Midian. Moses, once a prince of Egypt, now lived as a humble shepherd, tending the flock of his father-in-law, Jethro. The grandeur of Pharaoh's palace was long behind him. Once clothed in fine linen and surrounded by power, Moses now wore the simple garments of a shepherd and wandered the barren wilderness, far from the life he had known.

Yet even here, God was preparing him. What seemed like a season of obscurity was shaping Moses' character for the calling ahead.

Then, on one of those seemingly ordinary days, everything changed. Moses noticed something unusual—a bush ablaze with fire, yet not consumed. Its flames crackled without devouring the branches. Curiosity drew him closer, his steps cautious, his heart pounding. As he approached, a voice pierced the air:

**"Moses, Moses!"** (Exodus 3:4, NIV)

Startled, he stopped in his tracks.

**"Do not come any closer,"** the voice said. **"Take off your sandals, for the place where you are standing is holy ground."** (Exodus 3:5, NIV)

In ancient cultures, removing one's sandals was a gesture of reverence and humility. God was showing Moses that this wilderness moment was not ordinary—it was sacred. The desert had become a sanctuary, and Moses was standing in the presence of the Almighty.

### From Wilderness to Destiny

God spoke with compassion and authority:

**"I have indeed seen the misery of my people in Egypt. I have heard them crying out because of their slave drivers, and I am concerned about their suffering. So I have come down to rescue them."** (Exodus 3:7–8, NIV)

For four hundred years, Israel had languished in Egypt, enslaved and oppressed. Now, God was setting His plan into motion. But His method was surprising: He would send Moses—the runaway prince, the hesitant shepherd, the man who doubted himself.

**"So now, go. I am sending you to Pharaoh to bring my people, the Israelites, out of Egypt."** (Exodus 3:10, NIV)

Moses was stunned. He immediately voiced his insecurities:

**"Who am I that I should go to Pharaoh and bring the Israelites out of Egypt?"** (Exodus 3:11, NIV)

**"What if they do not believe me or listen to me?"** (Exodus 4:1, NIV)

**"I have never been eloquent... I am slow of speech and tongue."** (Exodus 4:10, NIV)

Excuse after excuse flowed from Moses' lips. His fear and self-doubt were louder than his faith.

But God answered every objection with reassurance:

**"I will be with you."** (Exodus 3:12, NIV)

And to prove His power, God gave Moses signs: a staff that turned into a serpent, a hand that became leprous and was healed again (Exodus 4:1-7, NIV). He even promised that Aaron, Moses' brother, would be his spokesman. God was making it clear. The calling was not about Moses' strength but about God's presence working through him.

## What Moses' Calling Teaches Us

Moses' encounter at the burning bush reminds us that God often chooses the hesitant and the humble for His most significant works. Like Moses, we may struggle with doubt:

We feel unqualified for the tasks before us.

We fear failure or rejection.

We question whether we truly heard God's call.

Yet God calls us anyway, not because we are fully ready, but because He is fully faithful. He equips those He sends, and His presence is our most excellent qualification.

*Where is God calling you to step forward in faith?*

*Are you allowing fear to hold you back?*

*Can you trust that He will provide everything you need for the mission ahead?*

## Prayer Prompt: Embracing Your Calling

Ask God to help you recognize and embrace the mission He has placed on your heart. Pray for courage to step forward despite fear, and for faith to trust that His presence will sustain you every step of the way.

---

### Community Reflection

- What excuses do we tend to make when we sense God calling us to something uncomfortable?

- How can we remind one another that God equips those He calls?

- Where do we see "burning bush" moments—ordinary places where God's presence breaks through—in our lives today?

---

## Final Reflections: God's Power in Our Weakness

The story of Moses at the burning bush reveals that God delights in calling the unlikely, the insecure, and the hesitant. Leadership in God's kingdom is not about human eloquence or ability but about surrender to His presence and power.

When doubts rise, His answer remains the same: **"I will be with you."** May we learn to lay down excuses, step forward in faith, and trust that God's strength is more than enough for every calling.

## 2.6 The Ten Plagues: Deliverance and Divine Power

Scripture Reference: Exodus 5:1–12:30

Imagine the scene: Moses, once a fugitive shepherd, now standing boldly in Pharaoh's royal court. The walls are adorned with gold, the air thick with incense, and the most powerful man in the known world sits on his throne. With Aaron by his side, Moses delivers the words God has given him:

**"This is what the Lord, the God of Israel, says: 'Let my people go, so that they may hold a festival to me in the wilderness.'"** (Exodus 5:1, NIV)

Pharaoh's reaction is swift and dismissive. **"Who is the Lord, that I should obey him and let Israel go? I do not know the Lord and I will not let Israel go."** (Exodus 5:2, NIV)

Laughter and defiance filled the court. Pharaoh's arrogance was not only a political stance. It was spiritual rebellion. And so began one of the most dramatic demonstrations of God's power in all of Scripture.

### Plague After Plague: A Battle of Divine Authority

Each plague that followed was not random. Every act struck directly at the heart of Egypt's gods, its culture, and its economy. What seemed like natural disasters were, in fact, a cosmic showdown between the one true God and the false deities Egypt trusted.

1. **The Nile turned to blood**, a direct blow to Egypt's river god, leaving the lifeline of their nation defiled (Exodus 7:14–24, NIV).

2. **Frogs swarmed the land**, mocking the gods of fertility who were powerless to control them (Exodus 8:1–15, NIV).

3. **Gnats covered people and animals**, invading every corner of daily life and defying Egypt's rituals of purity (Exodus 8:16–19, NIV).

4. **Flies filled every home and palace**, spreading filth and reminding Egypt that their gods of protection were powerless (Exodus 8:20–32, NIV).

5. **Livestock perished**, weakening Egypt's economy and striking at gods associated with bulls and cattle (Exodus 9:1–7, NIV).

6. **Painful boils afflicted the people**, reminding them that not even their bodies were beyond God's reach (Exodus 9:8–12, NIV).

7. **Hailstorms pounded the crops and fields**, demonstrating that Egypt's sky gods were powerless before the Creator (Exodus 9:13–35, NIV).

8. **Locusts devoured everything that remained**, leaving desolation where once there had been plenty (Exodus 10:1–20, NIV).

9. **Thick darkness covered the land for three days**, a direct challenge to Ra, Egypt's sun god (Exodus 10:21–29, NIV).

10. **Finally, the firstborn sons of Egypt died in a single night**—the ultimate judgment that revealed the futility of Pharaoh's power (Exodus 12:29–30, NIV).

Through it all, Pharaoh's heart remained hardened. Each refusal exposed the danger of pride: when a ruler exalted himself above God, he was ultimately brought low.

## The First Passover: A Covenant of Protection

Before the final plague, God gave His people clear instructions:

**"Take a lamb for your family, without defect... Slaughter it at twilight. Take some of the blood and put it on the sides and tops of the doorframes."** (Exodus 12:3, 5, 7, NIV)

That night, as the angel of death passed through Egypt, every home marked with the blood of the lamb was spared. Israel's deliverance came not through their strength but through God's covering.

This was not merely protection. It was the beginning of a covenant. The first Passover foreshadowed the sacrifice of Jesus Christ, the Lamb of God, whose blood would bring salvation and deliverance for all who believe (John 1:29, NIV).

## What the Plagues Teach Us About Deliverance

The story of the plagues is more than an account of ancient miracles. It is a reminder for us today that:

God hears the cries of the oppressed (Exodus 3:7, NIV).

No earthly power is greater than His authority.

Deliverance may come through struggle, but it is always certain in God's timing.

Just as Israel longed for freedom from Pharaoh's chains, we, too, wrestle with forces that enslave us—fear, addiction, shame, unforgiveness, or even the relentless pressure of our own ambitions. The plagues remind us that God is mighty to deliver, not only from external oppressors but also from the inner Pharaohs of our hearts.

*Where do you need deliverance in your life?*

*What "Pharaoh" is holding you captive?*

*Are you ready to trust God's promise of freedom?*

## Prayer Prompt: Trusting in God's Deliverance

Ask God to reveal the areas of your life where you need freedom. Pray for the faith to endure His process of deliverance, even if it comes through struggle. Thank Him for the Lamb whose blood has already secured your salvation.

**Community Reflection**

- How does Pharaoh's hardened heart serve as a warning about resisting God's voice?

- In what ways do we see "modern Pharaohs"—systems, habits, or struggles that enslave people—today?

- How can we support one another in walking toward freedom in Christ?

## Final Reflections: A God Who Calls and Saves

From the burning bush to the plagues of Egypt, Moses' story shows us that God's power is greater than any human authority. He calls us even when we feel unqualified. He is sovereign over all things, from the most minor details of life to the mightiest empires.

Deliverance is not only about escape. It is about entering into God's greater purpose. When He calls, when He delivers, when He leads, we are never the same.

May we step forward in faith, trusting His justice and embracing the freedom He offers, remembering that His power is not only to bring us out of bondage but to lead us into life with Him.

# Chapter 3

# Exodus and Covenant

T here was a season in my life when I faced a decision so daunting it felt like standing at the edge of an ocean with no bridge in sight. Fear whispered that I was trapped, hemmed in by uncertainty. I wondered if I would ever find a way forward or if the tide of doubt would sweep me away.

In that moment, I thought of the Israelites, cornered between Pharaoh's army and the Red Sea. Their story became my story. Like them, I needed faith not only to hope for deliverance but to step forward when no path was visible.

The story of the Red Sea is not just about God's power over nature. It is about His power to make a way in our lives when every option seems closed.

## 3.1 Crossing the Red Sea: Faith in Action

Scripture Reference: Exodus 14:1–31; Hebrews 11:29

The Israelites stood at the edge of disaster.

Before them, the endless waters of the Red Sea, waves churning and horizon unbroken. Behind them, the dust of Pharaoh's chariots rose into the air as his army thundered forward, intent on dragging them back into slavery. Trapped between two impossibilities, the people could have succumbed to despair. But they didn't.

They cried out, not in defeat, but in a plea for help:

**"Was it because there were no graves in Egypt that you brought us to the desert to die?"** (Exodus 14:11, NIV)

Fear clouded their vision. In their panic, the chains of Egypt almost looked safer than the uncertainty of freedom.

But Moses, standing firm in trust, raised his voice above the chaos and declared:

**"Do not be afraid. Stand firm and you will see the deliverance the Lord will bring you today... The Lord will fight for you; you need only to be still."** (Exodus 14:13–14, NIV)

Then, with nothing but a staff in his hand and faith in his heart, Moses stretched out his arm over the sea.

## The Miracle of the Waters

A mighty wind blew through the night. The waters trembled, parted, and rose into towering walls on either side. Dry ground appeared where there had been only deep waters moments before (Exodus 14:21–22, NIV).

The Israelites stepped forward, walking through the sea as if it were a valley carved just for them. Each step was more than movement—it was faith in action. Behind them, the chains of Egypt were breaking. Before them, a new identity was forming.

When the last Israelite reached the far shore, the waters returned with violent force, swallowing Pharaoh's army and silencing the threat once and for all (Exodus 14:27–28, NIV). God had fought for His people, and He had won.

## Faith Under Pressure

The Red Sea crossing was more than escape. It was a lesson in trust. Israel's faith was not perfect. They doubted. They complained. They hesitated. But even so, they walked forward. And God honored their step of faith.

The author of Hebrews later reflected: "**By faith the people passed through the Red Sea as on dry land.**" (Hebrews 11:29, NIV)

Sometimes faith is not about being fearless. It is about stepping forward while fear is still present, trusting that God is stronger than our doubts.

## What Is Your Red Sea?

We all face Red Sea moments—times when the obstacle ahead looks impassable, and retreat feels tempting.

A health diagnosis that shakes us to the core.

A financial burden that feels impossible to bear.

A relationship fractured beyond repair.

A dream so big it feels unreachable.

The Red Sea reminds us that what looks like a dead end may, in fact, be the very place where God reveals His power.

*What if your Red Sea isn't a barrier but a doorway?*

*What if the impossible is only waiting for you to take a step?*

*What if deliverance is already unfolding, even if you cannot yet see it?*

## Prayer Prompt: Your Red Sea

Bring before God the challenges that feel like walls of water towering over you. Tell Him your fears and your doubts. Ask Him for the courage to step forward in trust, believing that He is already at work in ways you cannot yet see.

Reflect on past seasons where God made a way for you, and let those memories strengthen your confidence that He will do it again.

Because you are not alone, the God who parted the Red Sea still parts the waters in our lives today. His intervention is not a one-time event, but a continuous act of love and grace.

---

### Community Reflection

- How do we respond when fear tempts us to see the past as safer than God's promises for the future?

- What are some modern "Red Seas" that seem impossible, and how can we face them together in faith?

- How can we remind each other of God's power when circumstances feel overwhelming?

---

## Final Reflections: Faith That Walks Forward

The crossing of the Red Sea is a powerful testament to the transformative power of faith. It shows us that deliverance is not only about freedom from the past but also about faith for the future. God transformed a group of formerly enslaved people into His covenant people through an act of power that silenced their oppressor and gave them a new identity.

May we remember that faith is not the absence of fear, but the courage to walk forward in the midst of it. When we face our Red Sea moments, may we trust the God who parts waters, makes a way where none exists, and calls us to step forward into His promises.

## 3.2 Manna from Heaven: Trusting God's Provision

Scripture Reference: Exodus 16:1–36

Imagine walking day after day through a wilderness where the horizon never changes. The sun beats down relentlessly, your feet ache from the sand and rocks, and the cries of hungry children echo in your ears. Every meal from Egypt is a fading memory—your body longs for bread, your spirit for hope.

This was the reality for the Israelites after leaving Egypt. Freedom had come at a cost: no fields to harvest, no markets to buy food, no crops to plant in the barren desert. Each day seemed to stretch further into uncertainty.

It is in this setting of need and desperation that God chose to reveal Himself as Provider. One morning, as the dew lifted from the ground, the people looked out and saw something astonishing. Small, thin flakes covering the earth like frost. They bent down, touched it, tasted it, and asked in bewilderment: **"What is it?"**

**"Manna,"** they called it, a word that literally means "What is it?" (Exodus 16:15, NIV). Bread from heaven.

Sweet like honey, gathered fresh each morning, just enough for the day. Can you imagine the awe they must have felt, witnessing this miraculous provision?

**"I will rain down bread from heaven for you. The people are to go out each day and gather enough for that day."** (Exodus 16:4, NIV)

For forty years, manna appeared with the sunrise, a daily reminder that their lives did not depend on their strength but on God's provision. In the emptiness of the wilderness, He became their sustainer.

### A Lesson in Faith and Obedience

God's instructions for manna were simple but profound:

Gather only what you need for the day.

On the sixth day, gather twice as much to prepare for the Sabbath.

Do not hoard or store it overnight.

Yet some, fearing tomorrow, tried to hold on to more than they needed. By morning, it spoiled, reeking with decay and crawling with maggots (Exodus 16:20, NIV). Their fear exposed the deeper struggle. Trusting that

God would provide again tomorrow. In contrast, those who obeyed found that manna was always enough.

Never too much. Never too little. This is the peace and security that comes from trust-driven obedience.

## The Sabbath Rest: A Test of Trust

A unique pattern emerged on the Sabbath. On the sixth day, they gathered double the portion, and unlike other days, it did not spoil.

God was teaching them to rest—not as an act of laziness, but as a declaration of faith.

Provision was never about control—it was about trust.

Rest was never about neglect—it was about reliance.

God's care extended beyond the work of their hands, inviting them to believe that even in stillness, He would sustain them.

## What Manna Teaches Us Today

We live in a culture that prizes accumulation. We save, store, and stockpile "just in case." We measure security by what we own rather than by who provides. But manna challenges that mindset.

Do we trust God to meet our needs one day at a time?

Do we live with open hands, or are we clinging tightly out of fear?

Do we practice rest, believing that God can sustain us even when we stop striving?

True contentment does not come from possessions. It comes from knowing the Provider.

## Prayer Prompt: Daily Gratitude

Each evening this week, pause to thank God for three blessings from your day. They might be as simple as a meal on the table, a moment of laughter, or a quiet pause amid busyness.

Ask Him to teach you to see His provision in both small mercies and great miracles. Let gratitude train your heart to trust Him daily, just as Israel learned in the wilderness.

Because the same God who sent manna each morning is providing for you today.

## Community Reflection

- Why do you think the Israelites struggled to trust God's daily provision?

- How do we see the same struggle in our own culture of "more"?

- What practices help us rest in God's care instead of grasping for control?

## Final Reflections: Enough for Today

The story of manna is more than bread from heaven. It is an invitation to live in daily dependence on God. He does not always give in abundance to silence our fears, but He always gives in sufficiency to strengthen our faith.

As we reflect on this story, may we learn to release our anxieties, embrace the rhythm of trust and rest, and find joy in the daily bread of His care. For just as He sustained His people in the wilderness, He sustains us now—enough for today, and enough for tomorrow.

## 3.3 The Golden Calf: Idolatry and Its Consequences

Scripture Reference: Exodus 32:1–35

The Israelites, on their journey of faith, had witnessed wonders unlike anything the world had ever seen. They had seen the Nile turned to blood, the plagues sweep through Egypt, the Red Sea split open before their eyes, and manna appear in the wilderness each morning. They had walked through miracles, led by a God who revealed Himself in fire and cloud.

And now, they were camped at Mount Sinai. The mountain shook with thunder, its peak wrapped in cloud and flame, a holy place where heaven seemed to touch earth. It was here that Moses had ascended, climbing into the presence of God to receive His law, the covenant that would shape Israel's identity as His chosen people.

At first, the people waited with reverence. Days passed. Then weeks. The mountaintop remained shrouded in smoke, but there was no sign of Moses returning. The silence grew heavy, and with each passing day, questions whispered through the camp. *Had the fire consumed Moses? Had God abandoned them? What would happen now?*

Their faith began to waver in the waiting. Fear, a natural human response, grew louder than trust. And in the absence of visible leadership, they turned to something they could see, something they could touch, something that gave the illusion of control.

**"As for this fellow Moses who brought us up out of Egypt, we don't know what has happened to him."** (Exodus 32:1, NIV)

This moment of fear opened the door to idolatry. Instead of trusting the unseen God who had delivered them, they longed for a tangible substitute.

### The Birth of the Golden Calf

Aaron, left in charge while Moses was on the mountain, faced mounting pressure. The people demanded something to worship, something to lead them forward. And Aaron gave in.

**"Take off the gold earrings... Bring them to me."** (Exodus 32:2, NIV)

The gold, given by God's provision when they left Egypt (Exodus 12:35–36, NIV), was melted down and formed into the image of a calf. In the cultures surrounding Israel, bulls and calves symbolized strength, fertility, and prosperity. The people were not inventing something new. They were returning to familiar symbols of power from Egypt and Canaan.

**"These are your gods, Israel, who brought you up out of Egypt."** (Exodus 32:4, NIV)

What was meant to be an offering of gratitude turned into a distortion of worship. The people celebrated with feasting, dancing, and sacrifice, exchanging the glory of the living God for an idol of their own making.

## Moses' Return: A Broken Covenant

When Moses descended the mountain, carrying the tablets inscribed with God's commandments, he was met not with reverence but with chaos. The people were dancing, feasting, and reveling around the golden calf. The covenant was already broken.

In anguish, Moses shattered the tablets (Exodus 32:19, NIV), a dramatic symbol of what the people had done. Judgment followed: the idol was destroyed, and those who led in rebellion faced death. A plague spread through the camp as a further consequence of disobedience (Exodus 32:35, NIV).

And yet, even here, mercy glimmered. Moses interceded for the people, pleading with God to forgive them.

God, who is **"compassionate and gracious, slow to anger, abounding in love and faithfulness"** (Exodus 34:6, NIV), relented.

This episode left an unshakable imprint on Israel's story: the dangers of idolatry and the depth of God's mercy.

## Recognizing Idolatry in Our Own Lives

The golden calf is more than an ancient event. It exposes a pattern we all face: turning God's gifts into gods themselves.

We may not melt gold into statues, but idolatry today looks like:

Placing success or career above faith.

Seeking comfort in possessions rather than God's presence.

Relying on human approval more than divine affirmation.

At its core, idolatry is about misplaced security. It asks: *What do I turn to when I feel anxious, uncertain, or afraid?*

## Realigning Our Devotion

The golden calf moment reminds us that:

*When we feel abandoned, God is still near.*

*When we feel out of control, He is still sovereign.*

*When we misplace our devotion, He invites us back.*

The lesson is not just to avoid idols but to learn how to wait faithfully. Instead of rushing to create substitutes, God calls us to trust His timing and presence.

## Prayer Prompt: Realigning Priorities

Ask God to reveal anything in your life that has taken His place. Pray for clarity to recognize subtle idols—whether control, approval, or comfort—and for the strength to surrender them. Invite Him to restore His rightful place at the center of your heart.

## Community Reflection

- Why do you think Israel chose a golden calf instead of waiting for God?

- What "golden calves" are most tempting in today's culture?

- How can we encourage one another to wait on God when patience runs thin?

## Final Reflections: Trust and Devotion

From manna in the wilderness to idols at Sinai, the contrast is clear: trust brings peace, impatience breeds chaos. The Israelites traded the invisible presence of God for a visible idol, but God's mercy called them back.

As we reflect on this story, may we:

Rest in the knowledge that God is always present, even in the waiting.

Please resist the temptation to place our security in what is temporary.

Return to Him again and again, knowing His grace never runs out.

Because faith is not only about believing. It is about trusting, waiting, and walking forward with God, even when His timing stretches our patience.

## 3.4 The Ten Commandments: Foundations of Moral Living

Scripture Reference: Exodus 19:1–20:21

The scene at Mount Sinai was unforgettable. The mountain stood tall against the desert horizon, its peak hidden in dense cloud and fire. Thunder rumbled, lightning split the sky, and a trumpet blast grew louder and louder until the people trembled with awe and fear (Exodus 19:16–19, NIV).

They had already witnessed the Red Sea part. They had seen manna fall from heaven. But here, at Sinai, God was not only showing His power. He was about to reveal His will. This moment was different. The Israelites were no longer simply a people rescued from slavery. They were being formed into a nation, set apart for a covenant relationship with the living God.

Moses ascended the mountain alone, stepping into the storm to meet with the Almighty. Every eye followed him upward. Every heart waited. What words would he bring down? What commands would define their identity as God's chosen people?

### The Law That Defined a Nation

From the mountaintop, surrounded by smoke and fire, God spoke words that would echo for generations—the Ten Commandments (Exodus 20:1–17, NIV). These were not arbitrary rules but the foundation of a covenant, binding God and His people in a relationship marked by love, holiness, and responsibility.

The commandments came in two great movements:

The first four focused on Israel's relationship with God, commanding devotion, reverence, and loyalty to Him alone.

The remaining six addressed life together as a community, emphasizing honor, honesty, justice, and respect.

**"You shall have no other gods before me."** (Exodus 20:3, NIV)

**"Honor your father and your mother."** (Exodus 20:12, NIV)

**"You shall not steal."** (Exodus 20:15, NIV)

The people stood at the foot of the mountain, trembling not only at the thunderous voice but at the weight of the words themselves. These laws were not meant to enslave them again but to set them free. They gave shape to their identity as a people who belonged to God.

In the ancient world, covenants were typical, often established between a king and his subjects. At Sinai, the Lord of creation, the one who had shattered Pharaoh's power, stooped to enter into a covenant with a community of formerly enslaved people. Unlike human rulers who demanded tribute, God gave dignity, order, and purpose. His commands offered a way of life that reflected His character.

## A Law That Still Shapes Us Today

The Ten Commandments did not fade with time. They became the backbone of moral and legal systems across history, inspiring justice, guiding ethics, and shaping human dignity. They were more than prohibitions; they were a vision of what it looks like to live rightly before God and with one another.

They continue to ask searching questions of us:

Are we honoring God with our devotion, or do other things compete for first place in our lives?

Are we treating others with the justice, honesty, and respect they deserve as fellow image-bearers of God?

Are we living with integrity when no one else is watching?

The Ten Commandments are not simply about following rules. They are about becoming the kind of people who reflect God's holiness and love in the world.

## Prayer Prompt: Living the Covenant

Ask God to write His commands on your heart. Pray for strength to honor Him in your daily decisions, wisdom to live with integrity, and love that flows into your relationships with others. Thank Him that His law is not meant to bind but to guide, leading us into the freedom of living as His people.

---

### Community Reflection

- Which of the commandments feels most challenging to live out in today's culture?

- How do these commands shape us as a community, not just as individuals?

- What practices help us honor both God and people in everyday life?

---

## Final Reflections: Covenant and Community

The Ten Commandments remind us that faith is never only personal. It is also communal. God's covenant at Sinai called Israel to devotion, justice, and integrity, not just for themselves but for the flourishing of the whole community.

As we reflect on this scene, we are invited to see these commands not as heavy chains but as guiding lights. They show us how to love God fully and how to love others rightly. They remind us that true freedom is not found in doing whatever we please, but in living within the covenant of the God who rescues, redeems, and restores.

Because in the end, the law is not about restriction, it is about relationship. It is the gift of a God who calls His people into holiness, not to burden them, but to bless them.

## 3.5 The Tabernacle: God's Dwelling Among His People

Scripture Reference: Exodus 25–40

The wilderness was harsh and unforgiving. The sun blazed during the day, the nights chilled to the bone, and the endless sands stretched as far as the eye could see. And yet, in that barren place, God asked His people to build something extraordinary.

Imagine the camp of Israel, thousands of tents spread across the desert floor, families busy with daily tasks, children running between rows of shelters. In the midst of ordinary life, a new project began to stir the people into action. Moses shared God's command:

**"Then have them make a sanctuary for me, and I will dwell among them."** (Exodus 25:8, NIV)

The people responded with eagerness. Men and women brought forward their most precious possessions:

Acacia wood, strong and enduring, is gathered from the sparse trees of the region.

Gold, silver, and bronze, once plundered from Egypt, now freely offered back to God.

Fine linens dyed scarlet, purple, and blue, woven with skill and care.

Gems and precious stones, to be set in the garments of the priests.

Each gift carried a story. Each item was more than material. It was devotion, surrender, and gratitude for the God who had delivered them. What once had symbolized wealth and security now became a contribution toward something far greater: **the Tabernacle, a dwelling place for the divine in the midst of His people** (Exodus 35:21–22, NIV).

Unlike the towering monuments of Egypt or the fortified palaces of kings, this sanctuary would not stand as a display of human power. It would be simple, portable, and sacred. A tent, not of human glory, but of God's presence. It was a reminder that the God who had split the Red Sea was not distant. He was near, choosing to live not above them, but among them.

## A Place for God Among His People

The Tabernacle was more than a structure. It was a sacred symbol of God's desire to dwell with His people. At its very center was the **Ark of the Covenant**, holding the tablets of the Ten Commandments, the tangible reminder of God's covenant with Israel (Exodus 25:21–22, NIV).

Surrounding the Ark was the **Holy of Holies**, a space so sacred that only the High Priest could enter, and only once a year on the Day of Atonement.

The golden **lampstand** (menorah) burned continually, its steady light symbolizing God's eternal presence (Exodus 27:20–21, NIV).

The **altar of incense** filled the space with fragrance, rising upward as a picture of the people's prayers carried to heaven (Exodus 30:7–8, NIV).

Every fabric, every measurement, every material was chosen with profound purpose. Nothing was random. Each element spoke of holiness, purity, and God's nearness.

Unlike the grand temples of Egypt or the fortified palaces of kings, God chose to dwell in a tent. Portable. Simple. Accessible. The God of creation humbled Himself to move with His people, reminding them that His presence was not bound to a single place but available wherever they went.

The people responded with such overflowing generosity that Moses eventually had to tell them to stop bringing more contributions, for they had already given more than enough (Exodus 36:6–7, NIV). The Tabernacle was built not only from materials but from willing hearts.

## Sacred Spaces in Our Own Lives

Even today, we long for places where we can encounter God. Sometimes it is a church sanctuary filled with song and prayer. Other times, it is a quiet corner in our homes where we kneel in solitude. Still other times, it is a walk in nature, where creation itself becomes a temple. It could also be a community service project, a family gathering, or a personal meditation spot.

The lesson of the Tabernacle is that God's presence is not limited to one sacred building. He delights to dwell wherever His people make room for Him. Sacred spaces are not only physical. They are created whenever we pause, invite God in, and recognize His presence with us.

Where in your life have you made space for God to dwell?

In the silence of prayer before the day begins?

Perhaps around the dinner table, when gratitude is offered before a meal.

Probably in the stillness of night, when worries are laid down at His feet.

Please take a moment to reflect on these spaces and how they have enriched your spiritual journey.

The Tabernacle reminds us that the holiest sanctuary is not made of wood and gold, but of hearts set apart for Him.

## Prayer Prompt: Welcoming God's Presence

Ask God to help you create sacred spaces in your daily life. Pray for a heart that welcomes His presence not only in moments of worship at church but also in ordinary rhythms—your work, your rest, your conversations. Thank Him for the gift of His nearness, and ask for eyes to notice it more fully.

---

### Community Reflection

- Why do you think God chose to dwell in a tent rather than a palace or temple?

- How do we, as a community, make space for God's presence today?

- What does it look like to give generously, as Israel did, to build spaces where God is honored?

## Final Reflections: God With Us

The Tabernacle stands as a potent reminder that God is not far away but near. He is not confined to temples of stone but delights to dwell among His people, even in the wilderness. Every detail of its design pointed to His holiness and His desire to be with those He loves.

As we reflect on this story, may we become a people who create sacred spaces in our lives, who give generously of ourselves, and who live with the assurance that His presence travels with us wherever we go.

Because the greatest gift of all is not merely God's provision. It is God Himself, dwelling with His people.

***

## 3.6 The Spies in Canaan: A Tale of Faith and Fear

Scripture Reference: Numbers 13:1–14:38

The wilderness journey had been long. After escaping Egypt, crossing the Red Sea, and receiving God's covenant at Sinai, the Israelites finally stood on the border of the land God had promised to their ancestors. The air must have been filled with both excitement and apprehension. Ahead of them lay Canaan, often described as a land flowing with milk and honey, the inheritance God had sworn to Abraham, Isaac, and Jacob.

At this critical moment, God gave Moses a command:

**"Send some men to explore the land of Canaan, which I am giving to the Israelites. From each ancestral tribe send one of its leaders."** (Numbers 13:1–2, NIV)

Twelve men were chosen, one from each tribe, entrusted with a mission that carried enormous weight. This was not only a reconnaissance mission to see what challenges lay ahead. It was a spiritual test to see whether

Israel would believe God's promises even when the obstacles seemed overwhelming.

## The Journey into Canaan

Imagine the spies as they set out, their sandals crunching over the rocky soil of a land both beautiful and intimidating. They moved silently through valleys and plains, observing the land's richness. Vineyards flourished, fields ripened with grain, and trees were heavy with fruit. In fact, the produce was so abundant that one cluster of grapes was so large it had to be carried on a pole between two men (Numbers 13:23, NIV).

But alongside the abundance, they also saw reasons for fear. Walled cities rose before them, guarded by strong armies. Among the inhabitants were men of great size and stature, warriors who made the spies feel small and powerless in comparison. The land was good, but it would not be easy.

After forty days of exploration, the spies returned to camp carrying both the fruit of the land and the weight of what they had seen. Their report divided the people and revealed a deep conflict between faith and fear.

## Faith versus Fear

Ten of the spies allowed fear to dominate their words. They admitted the land was good but declared that its people were too strong, its cities too fortified, its giants too overwhelming. **"We seemed like grasshoppers in our own eyes, and we looked the same to them."** (Numbers 13:33, NIV)

Two men, Caleb and Joshua, saw the same challenges but spoke from a different perspective. They acknowledged the strength of the enemy, yet their confidence was in the God who had already delivered Israel through the sea and sustained them with manna. Caleb urged the people, **"We should go up and take possession of the land, for we can certainly do it."** (Numbers 13:30, NIV) Joshua added that if the Lord were pleased with them, He would give them the land as promised (Numbers 14:8, NIV). Their courage in the face of fear is a testament to the power of faith.

But the voices of ten outweighed the voices of two. The people wept, grumbled, and rebelled. Fear clouded their memory of God's faithfulness. In despair, they even cried, **"If only we had died in Egypt! Or in this**

**wilderness!"** (Numbers 14:2, NIV). Their fear led to a tragic consequence: they would not enter the promised land. This is a stark reminder of the power of fear and the importance of choosing faith.

Because of their unbelief, God decreed that this generation would wander the wilderness for forty years, one year for every day the spies explored the land (Numbers 14:34, NIV). Only Caleb and Joshua, the two who trusted, would live to see the fulfillment of God's promise.

## What Giants Do You See?

The story of the spies is not only Israel's history, it is also our story. We, too, stand at the edge of our own "promised lands," called to trust God in the face of intimidating challenges.

For the Israelites, the giants were literal warriors. For us, the giants often take other forms. A diagnosis that leaves us fearful of the future. A financial burden that feels impossible to overcome. A broken relationship that seems beyond repair. A dream or calling that feels far too big for our own strength. These are the 'giants' we face today, and like the Israelites, we are called to face them with faith, not fear.

Fear whispers that we are too small and the challenge is too great. Faith reminds us that the God who has carried us this far will not abandon us now.

## Stepping Forward in Faith

The spies show us that faith does not deny the presence of obstacles but chooses to believe in God's power above them. Caleb and Joshua did not ignore the fortified cities or the giants. They thought that God was greater. This is a powerful reminder that faith is not naïve; it is confident in the One who has already proven Himself faithful. It is this faith that can help us overcome even the most daunting challenges.

Like Israel, we must choose which voice we will follow. Fear will keep us wandering in circles, but faith will lead us forward into the promises of God. This choice is ours to make, and it is a powerful one that can shape our journey.

## Prayer Prompt: Choosing Faith Over Fear

Bring before God a situation in your life where fear feels louder than faith. Ask Him to silence the lies that tell you that you are too weak or too small, that the situation is hopeless, or that God is not with you. Pray for the courage of Caleb and Joshua, to see obstacles not as barriers but as opportunities to trust His power.

---

### Community Reflection

- Why do you think the people found fear more convincing than faith?

- What are some "giants" we face in today's world, and how can we respond like Caleb and Joshua?

- How does remembering God's past faithfulness help us face current challenges?

---

## Final Reflections: A Call to Trust

From Mount Sinai to the border of Canaan, the Israelites' journey reveals the tension between faith and fear. The Ten Commandments taught them how to live. The Tabernacle reminded them that God dwelt among them.

And the spies revealed the choice that every generation must make: to walk in fear or to walk in faith.

As we reflect on these stories, we are invited to ask ourselves: What is shaping my decisions? Where am I making space for God's presence? Am I listening to the voice of fear, or to the voice of faith?

The Promised Land may look daunting, but it is never beyond God's reach. He is calling us to trust, to step forward, and to believe that His promises are true. The story is still being written, and the God who parted the sea and provided manna is the same God who calls us to walk into His promises today.

*Chapter 4*

# Judges and Kings

I remember sitting on the living room floor as a child, surrounded by scattered toys, as my grandmother, steady, gentle, and filled with unwavering faith, shared stories of remarkable figures from the Bible. Her voice carried both tenderness and authority, and through her storytelling, the people of Scripture seemed to step into our living room as if they were alive before us.

Among all the stories she told, one always stood out to me: **the story of Deborah**. Hers wasn't just another tale of war and victory; it was a story of wisdom, courage, and unexpected empowerment. Deborah was unlike the heroes I had heard about in Sunday school. She wasn't a warrior with a sword or a king sitting on a throne. She was a prophetess, a judge, and a leader whose strength came not from physical might but from faith, discernment, and courage.

At a time when leadership was reserved for men, Deborah's position was groundbreaking, even unsettling to the culture around her. And yet, her story gave hope to anyone who had ever felt unseen or unqualified. To hear about a woman sitting under a palm tree, rendering judgments and guiding a nation, was to realize that human expectations never confine God's calling.

Her story compels us to rethink what leadership looks like. It challenges us to see that wisdom and courage are not bound by tradition or gender.

It reminds us that God delights in raising leaders from unexpected places—people who rely on His strength rather than their own.

Deborah's wisdom and courage shine as beacons of light in a world often clouded by conformity. She was a woman who listened when others doubted, who stood firm when others hesitated, and who reminded Israel that victory comes not by might, but by trust in the Lord.

*** 

## 4.1 Deborah: A Leader Beyond Expectations

Scripture Reference: Judges 4:1–24; Judges 5:1–31

The story of Deborah takes us into one of the darkest seasons in Israel's history. For twenty long years, the people groaned under the cruel oppression of Jabin, king of Canaan, and his ruthless commander Sisera, whose nine hundred iron chariots terrorized the land (Judges 4:2–3, NIV). Iron weaponry was the height of military power in the ancient Near East, making Sisera's army seem untouchable. Villages were abandoned, roads were unsafe, and the people lived in constant fear (Judges 5:6–7, NIV).

And it is into this backdrop of despair that Deborah emerges. The text introduces her with striking simplicity:

**"Now Deborah, a prophet, the wife of Lappidoth, was leading Israel at that time. She held court under the Palm of Deborah... and the Israelites went up to her to have their disputes decided"** (Judges 4:4–5, NIV).

Here was something extraordinary. In a culture where men dominated positions of authority, Deborah was recognized as both a prophetess who spoke God's word and a judge who delivered wisdom and justice. She did not sit on a throne or rule from a fortress but under a palm tree—open, approachable, and trusted by her people. Her authority did not come from convention but from the hand of God Himself.

## The Call to Battle

Israel's cries of despair did not go unheard. In their desperation, God spoke through Deborah, and she summoned Barak, a seasoned leader from Kedesh in Naphtali. Her words carried divine authority, not personal ambition:

**"Go, take with you ten thousand men of Naphtali and Zebulun and lead them up to Mount Tabor. I will lead Sisera, the commander of Jabin's army, with his chariots and his troops to the Kishon River and give him into your hands"** (Judges 4:6–7, NIV).

For Barak, the command must have felt overwhelming. Sisera's army was not just strong. It was unmatched. His nine hundred iron chariots thundered across the plains, symbols of unstoppable power in the ancient world.

Against such a force, Israel's ragtag militia of farmers and shepherds seemed hopeless.

Barak's hesitation was not cowardice but human calculation. He replied honestly: he would only go if Deborah went with him (Judges 4:8, NIV). This response revealed both his fear and his faith. He knew Deborah was no ordinary leader; her presence meant God Himself was going with them.

Deborah agreed, but her response was both encouraging and prophetic:

**"Certainly I will go with you. But because of the course you are taking, the honor will not be yours, for the Lord will deliver Sisera into the hands of a woman"** (Judges 4:9, NIV).

Her words pointed to a surprising twist. In a world where honor belonged to kings and warriors, God was preparing to work through the unexpected once again.

## The Victory at Mount Tabor

The day of battle arrived. From the high slopes of Mount Tabor, Israel's ten thousand men looked down upon Sisera's mighty army spread across the valley floor. The ground trembled under the weight of iron chariots, their polished weapons gleaming in the sun. Against such force, Israel appeared hopelessly outmatched.

But Deborah's faith never wavered. At the crucial moment, she declared with boldness:

**"Go! This is the day the Lord has given Sisera into your hands. Has not the Lord gone ahead of you?"** (Judges 4:14, NIV).

Barak charged down the mountain, and what followed was nothing short of divine intervention. A sudden storm swept across the valley, turning the Kishon River into a raging torrent (Judges 5:20–21, NIV). The ground, once firm, dissolved into mud. The great advantage of Sisera's army—their iron chariots—became their downfall, stuck and useless in the mire.

The Israelites surged forward, and Scripture records, **"At Barak's advance, the Lord routed Sisera and all his chariots and army by the sword"** (Judges 4:15, NIV). Panic spread, soldiers scattered, and Sisera himself abandoned his chariot, fleeing on foot into the wilderness.

## Jael: An Unexpected Heroine

Sisera's flight led him to the tent of Jael, the wife of Heber the Kenite. To Sisera, Jael appeared harmless. She welcomed him warmly, offered him milk to drink, and invited him to rest. Exhausted from battle, he collapsed in her tent, certain he had found safety.

But Jael was not passive. As he slept, she took the tools of her daily life—a tent peg and a hammer—and with courage and precision, she drove the peg through his temple into the ground (Judges 4:21, NIV). The mighty commander fell, not at the hands of a warrior, but at the hands of a woman whose boldness fulfilled Deborah's prophecy.

In that moment, God's word came true. Victory did not belong to Barak or to Israel's army but to God, working through Deborah's leadership and Jael's unexpected courage.

## Deborah's Song

In the aftermath of victory, Deborah's voice rose again, not in command, but in song. Alongside Barak, she composed one of the oldest hymns in Scripture, preserved in Judges 5. Her song celebrated God's triumph, honored the willing, and reminded Israel of the power of obedience:

**"When the princes in Israel take the lead, when the people willingly offer themselves—praise the Lord!"** (Judges 5:2, NIV).

The song looked beyond human strength and credited the victory entirely to God:

"From the heavens the stars fought, from their courses they fought against Sisera. The river Kishon swept them away" (Judges 5:20–21, NIV).

This was more than poetry; it was theology in song. It declared that God rules over creation, that He fights for His people, and that He works through the willing, however unexpected they may be.

---

### Community Reflection

- Which part of the armor of God do you find most difficult to "put on" consistently, and why?

- How can we, as a church or small group, support one another in staying spiritually strong and alert?

- What everyday practices can help us recognize and resist subtle distractions or compromises that weaken faith?

---

## Why Deborah's Story Still Matters

Deborah's story still speaks powerfully to us today. She challenges cultural assumptions, reminding us that leadership is not confined to gender, pedigree, or social status. God's call equips those He chooses, and His power flows through faith and obedience.

Her wisdom shows that authentic leadership is rooted in discernment, courage, and devotion to God's word. Her courage demonstrates that faith can rally a people in despair. Jael's bold act reminds us that God often uses ordinary tools and unexpected people to accomplish extraordinary purposes.

*** 

## 4.2 Gideon's Victory: Strength in Weakness

Scripture Reference: Judges 6:1–7:25

Israel was in a dark season. The Midianites, a nomadic people, had become a relentless scourge. They swept into the land like locusts, devouring crops, stealing livestock, and leaving devastation in their wake. The Israelites, once confident in God's promises, now hid in caves and mountain strongholds, afraid to live openly in their own land (Judges 6:1–6, NIV).

It is here, in the shadow of oppression, that we first meet Gideon.

Picture him crouched low, threshing wheat not on the open threshing floor where the wind could carry away the chaff, but in the hidden confines of a winepress. It was an act of survival, not strategy. Gideon was not preparing for war. He was trying to scrape together food without drawing Midianite attention (Judges 6:11, NIV).

And then, in the midst of his fear and secrecy, the angel of the Lord appeared and spoke words that seemed almost laughable:

**"The Lord is with you, mighty warrior."** (Judges 6:12, NIV)

Mighty warrior? Gideon hardly felt like one. His response revealed his doubt and insecurity:

**"Pardon me, my lord,"** Gideon replied, **"but how can I save Israel? My clan is the weakest in Manasseh, and I am the least in my family."** (Judges 6:15, NIV)

By every human measure, Gideon was unqualified. But God does not see as humans see. He does not call the qualified—He qualifies the called.

## A Test of Faith

Though God promised to be with him, Gideon wrestled with doubt. Could this really be God's will? To strengthen his faith, he asked for signs. First, he laid a fleece on the ground. If the fleece were wet with dew while the ground was dry, he would believe. God answered. The next night, he reversed the test: the fleece remained dry while the ground was soaked (Judges 6:36–40, NIV).

These signs revealed Gideon's uncertainty, but they also revealed God's patience. God accepted Gideon's weakness; He met him in it, nurturing his faith step by step, showing us that God understands our doubts and is patient with us as we grow in faith.

## An Impossible Battle Plan

When the time for battle came, Gideon summoned 32,000 men. It was a modest force compared to Midian's vast army, but it was something. Yet God declared it too many:

**"You have too many men. I cannot deliver Midian into their hands, or Israel would boast against me, 'My own strength has saved me.'"** (Judges 7:2, NIV)

First, 22,000 fearful men departed, leaving 10,000 (Judges 7:3, NIV). Still too many, God said. By the time God finished refining the army, only 300 remained (Judges 7:6–7, NIV).

In the ancient world, victory was measured by numbers and weapons. But here, God stripped away every illusion of self-reliance. The coming victory would not belong to Israel's might, but to God's power.

## Victory Against All Odds

Armed with torches hidden in clay jars, trumpets in hand, and faith in their hearts, Gideon's 300 surrounded the Midianite camp under the cover of night. At Gideon's signal, they shattered the jars, raised their torches, and blew the trumpets, crying out:

**"A sword for the Lord and for Gideon!"** (Judges 7:20, NIV)

Panic spread through the enemy camp. Confusion turned ally against ally:

**"The Lord caused the men throughout the camp to turn on each other with their swords."** (Judges 7:22, NIV)

What should have been an impossible battle ended in overwhelming victory, not because of human strength, but because of divine intervention.

## Faith Over Fear

Gideon's story still speaks with power today. His journey from fear to faith reminds us that:

God often calls the unlikely to accomplish His work.

Our weakness is not a disqualification—it is the stage where God's strength is revealed (2 Corinthians 12:9, NIV).

Faith does not mean we never doubt, but that we step forward anyway, trusting God's promises.

Like Gideon, we often feel too small, too weak, too unqualified. Yet God delights in using what seems insignificant to achieve the impossible.

## Prayer Prompt: Strength in Weakness

Bring before God an area of your life where you feel weak or unqualified. Pray for courage to step out in faith, trust in His power instead of your own, and humility to let Him work through your weakness.

## Community Reflection

- Why do you think God reduced Gideon's army instead of allowing the 32,000 to fight (Judges 7:2–7, NIV)?

- How do Gideon's doubts mirror our own struggles with faith?

- What "torches and trumpets" has God placed in your hands—unexpected tools that He can use for His glory?

## Final Reflections: God's Power in Our Weakness

Gideon's victory shows us that God delights in using the unlikely to accomplish the impossible. Our weakness is not a barrier. It is an invitation for His strength to shine.

When we feel insignificant, God calls us mighty. When we feel overwhelmed, He reminds us that He goes before us. When the odds seem stacked against us, He shows us that the battle belongs to Him.

May we, like Gideon, learn to see ourselves as God sees us, step forward in faith even when fear lingers, and trust that His power is enough for every battle.

Because **"The Lord is with you, mighty warrior"** (Judges 6:12, NIV)—and that changes everything.

## 4.3 Samson's Downfall: The Cost of Compromise

Scripture Reference: Judges 13:1–16:31

The story of Samson begins with a divine promise, a beacon of hope in a dark time. Israel was once again under the heavy hand of the Philistines, who oppressed them with cruelty and control (Judges 13:1, NIV). But into this darkness, God miraculously raised a deliverer, Samson.

An angel appeared to a barren woman, announcing that she would bear a son who would begin to save Israel. But this child was to be different. Set apart from birth as a Nazarite, consecrated to God's service (Judges 13:3–5, NIV). The vow included three commands: no wine or strong drink, no contact with the dead, and no cutting of his hair. These outward signs symbolized an inward devotion to God.

From the very beginning, Samson's life was marked by an extraordinary purpose. He was chosen, consecrated, and empowered. His parents raised him in obedience to this calling, and **"the Spirit of the Lord began to stir him"** as he grew (Judges 13:24–25, NIV).

Yet, as we soon learn, a great calling does not protect from human weakness.

### A Life of Strength and Weakness

Samson's exploits made him legendary. Scripture records astonishing feats:

He tore apart a lion with his bare hands (Judges 14:6, NIV).

He struck down 1,000 Philistines using only a donkey's jawbone (Judges 15:15, NIV).

He carried away the massive gates of Gaza on his shoulders, a humiliating blow to his enemies (Judges 16:3, NIV).

These victories showed the Spirit of God at work through him. But alongside his strength ran a reckless pattern of indulgence. Samson was often driven not by faith or justice, but by impulse and desire, particularly in his attraction to Philistine women, which repeatedly placed him in danger and compromised his calling.

His greatest weakness, however, came in his entanglement with Delilah.

## The Betrayal of Delilah

The Philistine rulers saw in Delilah the perfect weapon. They bribed her to uncover the source of Samson's strength (Judges 16:5, NIV).

Again and again, she asked:

**"Tell me the secret of your great strength and how you can be tied up and subdued."** (Judges 16:6, NIV)

Samson toyed with her, giving false answers. But eventually, his arrogance and carelessness led to a devastating confession:

**"No razor has ever been used on my head... If my head were shaved, my strength would leave me, and I would become as weak as any other man."** (Judges 16:17, NIV)

As he slept, Delilah had his hair cut. When Samson awoke, expecting to fight as before, he discovered the most chilling reality:

**"But he did not know that the Lord had left him."** (Judges 16:20, NIV)

Captured. Blinded. Shackled. Samson—the mighty warrior set apart from birth—was now a prisoner grinding grain in the enemy's prison.

## A Final Redemption

Yet even in judgment, God's grace was not absent. Samson's hair began to grow again (Judges 16:22, NIV), a quiet sign that his story was not yet finished. This is a powerful reminder that even in our lowest moments, redemption is possible.

Brought out to entertain the Philistines in their temple, Samson prayed one last desperate prayer:

**"Sovereign Lord, remember me. Please, God, strengthen me just once more."** (Judges 16:28, NIV)

Placing his hands on the temple pillars, he pushed with renewed strength. The structure collapsed, killing Samson and thousands of

Philistines with him (Judges 16:29–30, NIV). His life ended in tragedy, yet his final act struck a fatal blow to Israel's enemies and fulfilled the purpose God had given him—to begin Israel's deliverance from Philistine rule.

## Lessons from Samson's Life

Samson's story is both inspiring and sobering.

**Small compromises lead to significant downfalls.** Samson treated his vow casually, and it cost him everything.

**Strength without wisdom is dangerous**. Physical might could not compensate for spiritual weakness.

**Even in failure, redemption is possible.** Samson's final prayer reminds us that God can use us even at our lowest.

His life compels us to ask:

*Are there compromises in our lives that could one day undo us?*

*Do we allow impulse to rule us, or do we live with purpose and discipline?*

*Are we trusting in our own strength, or in God's?*

Samson's downfall is a warning, but also a testimony: even when we falter, God's mercy can bring redemption.

## Prayer Prompt: Guarding Against Compromise

Ask God to reveal areas of compromise in your life. Pray for wisdom to recognize temptations early, strength to resist them, and integrity to live faithfully. Thank Him that even when you stumble, His grace is greater than your failure.

---

**Community Reflection**

- Why do you think Samson's weaknesses eventually overcame his strengths (Judges 16:4–21, NIV)?

- What compromises are most tempting in today's world, and how can we guard against them?

- How does Samson's final prayer give hope to those who feel they've failed (Judges 16:28, NIV)?

---

## Final Reflections: Strength in Surrender

From Gideon's unlikely victory to Samson's tragic downfall, the book of Judges reveals the same truth: human strength is fragile, but God's strength never fails. Samson's compromises led to his destruction, but his surrender led to redemption.

His story reminds us that compromise destroys, but surrender redeems. Even in weakness, God can restore and use us for His purposes.

May we guard our hearts, live with integrity, and remember that our greatest strength is not found in ourselves but in God alone.

***

## 4.4 Ruth's Loyalty: Love and Redemption

Scripture Reference: Ruth 1:1–4:22

In the days when the judges ruled, Israel was caught in a cycle of disobedience, hardship, and deliverance. It was a time of instability and moral decline (Judges 21:25, NIV). Yet, in the midst of this turbulent era, the book of Ruth tells a very different story.

It is not a tale of kings, battles, or prophets. Instead, it is the story of two widows—Naomi and Ruth—and how their faithfulness and love became the foundation of redemption and legacy. It is an intimate story of ordinary people, ordinary struggles, and an extraordinary God weaving His purposes through acts of loyalty, courage, and grace.

## Ruth's Choice: A Declaration of Faith

Ruth's story begins with loss. Naomi, her Israelite mother-in-law, had moved with her husband and sons to Moab during a famine. But in Moab, Naomi's husband and both sons died, leaving Naomi and her daughters-in-law widowed (Ruth 1:1–5, NIV).

Naomi decided to return to Bethlehem and urged Ruth and Orpah, her daughters-in-law, to remain in Moab, where they might remarry and rebuild their lives. Orpah reluctantly agreed, but Ruth clung to Naomi. Her words echo through history as one of the most profound declarations of loyalty and faith:

**"Where you go, I will go, and where you stay, I will stay. Your people will be my people, and your God my God."** (Ruth 1:16, NIV)

This was more than loyalty to Naomi. Ruth, a Moabite by birth, was declaring her faith in the God of Israel. She chose not only Naomi but also Naomi's people and Naomi's God.

## Gleaning in the Fields of Boaz

When Ruth and Naomi arrived in Bethlehem, they had little more than hope. To survive, Ruth went to glean in the fields, gathering leftover grain after the harvesters. This practice, commanded by God in the law, ensured provision for the poor and the foreigner:

**"When you reap the harvest of your land, do not reap to the very edges of your field or gather the gleanings of your harvest. Leave them for the poor and for the foreigner residing among you."** (Leviticus 23:22, NIV)

Ruth's diligence and humility brought her to the field of Boaz, a wealthy and respected landowner. Boaz noticed her, not merely for her appearance, but for her kindness and devotion to Naomi.

**"I've been told all about what you have done for your mother-in-law since the death of your husband... May the Lord repay you for what you have done."** (Ruth 2:11–12, NIV)

Boaz protected her, instructed his workers to provide for her, and ensured that Ruth's efforts were honored. A simple act of gathering grain became the beginning of redemption.

## The Kinsman-Redeemer

Through Naomi's guidance, Ruth approached Boaz at the threshing floor, a symbolic request for marriage under the custom of the **kinsman-redeemer**. In Israelite law, a close relative could marry a widow to preserve the family's inheritance and continue its name (Ruth 3:9, NIV).

Boaz, impressed by Ruth's character and faith, agreed. He first ensured that the nearer relative declined his right, then married Ruth in a covenant of honor and love (Ruth 4:9–10, NIV).

Their union produced a son, Obed, who became the grandfather of King David (Ruth 4:17, NIV). In this way, Ruth—a Moabite outsider—was woven into the lineage of Jesus Christ (Matthew 1:5, NIV).

## Lessons from Ruth's Loyalty

Ruth's story teaches timeless truths:

Loyalty is not born from obligation, but from love and faith.

God works through ordinary acts of kindness to accomplish extraordinary purposes.

Steadfast commitment can transform not only our own lives but generations to come.

Her decision to follow Naomi and her God brought hope to a grieving widow, redemption to her family, and ultimately a blessing to the entire world through the line of Christ.

## Living Out Ruth's Faith Today

Ruth's faith invites us to ask:

*Are we practicing loyalty and devotion in our closest relationships?*

*Do we trust God when we are in unfamiliar or uncertain places?*

*Are we willing to see His providence at work in small, everyday acts of love?*

## Prayer Prompt: Trusting in God's Plan

Ask God to help you embrace faithfulness in your relationships and to trust His unseen hand in your circumstances. Pray for courage to step forward when the future feels uncertain and for eyes to see His provision in ordinary places.

### Community Reflection

- How does Ruth's loyalty challenge our view of commitment in relationships today (Ruth 1:16–17, NIV)?

- In what ways can we create modern "gleaning spaces"—acts of generosity that support the vulnerable in our communities (Leviticus 23:22, NIV)?

- What does Ruth's inclusion in the lineage of Jesus teach us about God's grace for outsiders (Matthew 1:5, NIV)?

## Final Reflections: Love That Redeems

Ruth's story is a beacon of hope. In a time of national chaos and personal loss, her loyalty and faith brought restoration, redemption, and a legacy that would shape salvation history.

Her devotion reminds us that God often works not through the powerful or the famous, but through the faithful choices of ordinary people.

May we, like Ruth, trust God in unfamiliar paths, honor our relationships with steadfast love, and believe that He is weaving our lives into His redemptive story.

Because faithfulness today can shape the generations of tomorrow.

***

## 4.5 Samuel's Call: Hearing God's Voice

Scripture Reference: 1 Samuel 1:1–3:21

The story of Samuel begins long before his first words to God. It starts with a woman's desperate prayer. Hannah, barren and brokenhearted, wept before the Lord in Shiloh, promising that if God gave her a son, she would dedicate him to His service for life (1 Samuel 1:10–11, NIV). God heard, and Samuel was born.

True to her vow, Hannah brought Samuel to Eli the priest when he was still a boy:

**"I prayed for this child, and the Lord has granted me what I asked of him. So now I give him to the Lord. For his whole life he will be given over to the Lord."** (1 Samuel 1:27–28, NIV)

From the beginning, Samuel's life was a gift, a living testimony to answered prayer and surrender.

He grew up in the tabernacle at Shiloh, serving under Eli. It was not an easy time in Israel's history. Spiritual corruption was rampant among Eli's sons, and Israel itself was drifting from God. Scripture notes, **"In those days the word of the Lord was rare; there were not many visions."** (1 Samuel 3:1, NIV). Against this backdrop of silence, God was about to speak through a child.

## The Night God Called

One night, as the temple lamps flickered and faded in the stillness, Samuel lay resting near the Ark of God. Suddenly, a voice pierced the silence:

**"Samuel!"** (1 Samuel 3:4, NIV)

Startled, the boy ran to Eli: **"Here I am; you called me."** But Eli shook his head. It was not he who called. Again and again the voice came, until Eli realized what was happening. He instructed the boy:

**"If He calls you, say, 'Speak, Lord, for your servant is listening.'"** (1 Samuel 3:9, NIV)

And so Samuel returned to his place. When the voice came again, Samuel responded with the words that would shape the rest of his life:

**"Speak, for your servant is listening."** (1 Samuel 3:10, NIV)

That night, God revealed His first message to Samuel—a hard word about judgment against Eli's household (1 Samuel 3:11–14, NIV).

Yet from this moment on, **"the Lord was with Samuel as he grew up, and He let none of Samuel's words fall to the ground."** (1 Samuel 3:19, NIV).

## Samuel: Judge, Prophet, and Kingmaker

Samuel's calling did not end at the temple that night. As he grew, he became the last of Israel's judges and the first of its great prophets. His role was foundational:

He called Israel back to faithfulness, urging them to turn away from idols (1 Samuel 7:3, NIV).

He interceded for the people, leading them in repentance and prayer.

He anointed Saul as Israel's first king (1 Samuel 10:1, NIV).

Later, he anointed David, the shepherd boy who would become "a man after God's own heart" (1 Samuel 16:13, NIV).

Samuel was a bridge between eras, from the chaos of the judges to the monarchy. But his leadership always flowed from one foundation: he first listened to God.

## Hearing and Responding to God's Voice

Samuel's call teaches timeless truths about faith:

God often speaks in unexpected ways, through people others might overlook.

Recognizing His voice requires attentiveness and obedience.

Authentic leadership is born not from ambition but from listening to God first.

## Are We Listening?

In our noisy, fast-paced lives, we often miss the quiet voice of God.

*Are we too distracted to notice His call?*

*Do we respond with obedience when we hear Him?*

*Are we open to being used in ways we do not feel prepared for?*

Samuel was a child in a time of spiritual silence. Yet he answered, and through him, God reshaped a nation.

## Prayer Prompt: Listening for God's Voice

Ask God to quiet the noise around you and within you. Pray for a heart that is attentive to His whispers, the humility to say **"Speak, Lord,"** and the courage to obey what He reveals.

---

**Community Reflection**

- Why do you think God chose to speak to a boy when "the word of the Lord was rare"? (1 Samuel 3:1, NIV)

- How can we train ourselves to discern God's voice amid the distractions of today?

- What role does obedience play after hearing God's call (1 Samuel 3:19, NIV)?

---

## Final Reflections: A Heart That Listens

Samuel's story reminds us that God does not always choose the expected person or speak in dramatic ways. Sometimes, He calls in the stillness of the night. Sometimes, He speaks to the overlooked. Samuel's response—simple, humble, and willing—set the trajectory for his life and for Israel's history.

May we learn to quiet our hearts, listen closely, and respond with the exact words of surrender:

**"Speak, Lord, for your servant is listening."** (1 Samuel 3:9–10, NIV)

***

## 4.6 David and Goliath: Facing Giants with Faith

Scripture Reference: 1 Samuel 17:1–58

The valley of Elah was alive with tension. Two armies stood on opposite hillsides, separated by a vast stretch of land. Israel's soldiers gripped their weapons but dared not move. Across the valley, the Philistines roared with confidence, their champion leading the taunts.

Goliath of Gath towered above every man, nearly ten feet tall, his bronze armor gleaming in the sun. His helmet and coat of scale armor alone weighed more than an ordinary soldier could carry. His spear's shaft was like a weaver's rod, its iron tip heavy enough to pierce through any shield (1 Samuel 17:4–7, NIV). Day after day, he stepped forward, his voice booming:

**"Choose a man and have him come down to me. If he can fight and kill me, we will become your subjects; but if I overcome him and kill him, you will become our subjects and serve us."** (1 Samuel 17:8–9, NIV)

Each time, fear rippled through Israel's camp. **"On hearing the Philistine's words, Saul and all the Israelites were dismayed and terrified"** (1 Samuel 17:11, NIV). No one dared answer.

Into this scene stepped David. He had not come as a soldier but as a shepherd boy, carrying bread and grain for his brothers. Yet as he listened to Goliath's insults against the living God, something rose within him. Where others saw only an invincible giant, David saw a battle that already belonged to the Lord.

## A Different Kind of Warrior

David was not trained for war. He was a shepherd, skilled with a sling but unfamiliar with sword and armor. When King Saul offered him armor, it weighed him down. He took it off, saying,

**"I cannot go in these, because I am not used to them."** (1 Samuel 17:39, NIV)

Instead, David chose what he knew: a shepherd's staff, a sling, and five smooth stones from the brook (1 Samuel 17:40, NIV).

To Goliath, the sight was laughable. **"Am I a dog, that you come at me with sticks?"** he sneered (1 Samuel 17:43, NIV).

But David's confidence did not waver. His faith was not in weapons but in the God who had delivered him before:

**"The Lord who rescued me from the paw of the lion and the paw of the bear will rescue me from the hand of this Philistine."** (1 Samuel 17:37, NIV)

And as he faced the giant, he declared with boldness:

**"You come against me with sword and spear and javelin, but I come against you in the name of the Lord Almighty."** (1 Samuel 17:45, NIV)

## Victory in the Unexpected

With steady hands, David loaded a stone into his sling and let it fly. The stone struck Goliath's forehead, sinking deep. The giant fell facedown to the ground (1 Samuel 17:49, NIV).

The battlefield fell silent. Then, a roar of victory broke out as the Israelites surged forward. What had seemed impossible was now reality. The boy-shepherd had slain the giant warrior.

This victory not only delivered Israel but also marked the beginning of David's rise. It revealed a truth that would define his kingship: true strength comes not from weapons or armies but from trusting in God.

## Lessons from David's Battle

David's encounter with Goliath teaches us timeless lessons:

Fear distorts, but faith clarifies. Israel saw an invincible enemy. David saw an opportunity to glorify God.

Victory comes through trust, not strength. David's sling was only a tool. Faith was the actual weapon.

Faith requires action. David did not wait for someone else to act. He stepped forward, trusting God to provide the victory.

We, too, face giants—challenges that loom large, whispering defeat before the battle even begins. But the question remains: will we measure our battles by human strength or by God's power?

## Facing Your Own Giants

What giants stand before you today? Fear, doubt, addiction, financial strain, broken relationships, or dreams that feel impossible? Like David, you may feel unprepared or outmatched. But God does not call the strongest. He strengthens those who are willing to trust Him.

Faith is not about having every answer. It is about stepping forward, even when the odds are stacked against you.

## Prayer Prompt: Trusting God in Battle

Bring before God the giant you are facing. Ask Him to shift your focus from fear to faith, from the size of the problem to the greatness of His power. Pray for courage to take the first step and for confidence to declare, as David did, that the battle belongs to the Lord (1 Samuel 17:47, NIV).

---

### Community Reflection

- Why do you think Saul and Israel's soldiers struggled to see what David saw (1 Samuel 17:11, NIV)?

- What "giants" in our communities seem overwhelming, and how might faith help us face them?

- How can we discern when God is calling us to step forward instead of waiting for someone else?

---

## Final Reflections: Faith That Faces Giants

David's story reminds us that courage is not the absence of fear but the choice to trust God when fear shouts loudest. His triumph over Goliath reveals that no obstacle is too significant when God is with us.

From Deborah's wisdom and Gideon's trust to Ruth's loyalty and Samuel's obedience, each story shows us what faith looks like in action. David's victory adds this truth: faith does not just see giants—it sees God, and that changes everything.

May we, like David, step forward with confidence, knowing that the same God who delivered him is with us today.

## << Scan the QR code to share your review >>

**THANK YOU**

\*\*\*

# Chapter 5

# Prophets and Prophecies

There are moments in history when silence feels deafening, when truth is ignored, and when people chase after empty promises. The prophets lived in such times. They were ordinary people called to carry an extraordinary message: a summons to return to God. Their courage in the face of opposition is a source of inspiration for us all.

Their stories are not only about predicting the future but also about the enduring nature of God's communication. They remind us that God still speaks. Sometimes His voice comes in whispers, sometimes in fire, but always with the power to draw us back to Him.

This chapter explores the lives of prophets who stood boldly for truth, revealed God's power through miracles, and reminded Israel and us that His word never fails.

## 5.1 Elijah on Mount Carmel: A Stand for Truth

Scripture Reference: 1 Kings 18:1–46

The land was dry, cracked, and silent. For three years, there had been no rain. Wells ran empty, fields turned to dust, and hunger gnawed at the people. It was as if the heavens themselves had closed. This drought was not random; it had come at the word of Elijah the prophet, who had declared that no rain would fall until God spoke again (1 Kings 17:1, NIV).

But the drought was more than a natural disaster. It was a spiritual crisis. King Ahab and Queen Jezebel had turned the hearts of Israel toward Baal, a Canaanite storm god believed to control rain and fertility. The silence of heaven was God's rebuke of this false worship.

Into this setting, Elijah emerged from hiding with a challenge that would decide the nation's future. On Mount Carmel, before the king, the prophets of Baal, and the gathered people of Israel, he demanded a choice.

**"How long will you waver between two opinions? If the Lord is God, follow him; but if Baal is God, follow him."** (1 Kings 18:21, NIV)

This was not just a contest of fire but a confrontation of loyalty. The people could no longer balance devotion to God with devotion to idols. They had to decide.

### The Test: Yahweh or Baal

Two altars were built. Two sacrifices are prepared. The true God would answer with fire.

From morning until evening, the 450 prophets of Baal cried out, leaping, dancing, and even cutting themselves to gain their God's attention. Yet despite all their efforts, there was only silence (1 Kings 18:26–29, NIV).

Then Elijah stepped forward. He repaired the altar of the Lord with twelve stones, symbolizing the twelve tribes of Israel (1 Kings 18:31, NIV). He arranged the wood, placed the bull upon it, and then did the unthinkable. He commanded water to be poured over the altar, not once but three times, until it ran down and filled the trench (1 Kings 18:33–35, NIV). Every natural possibility of fire was eliminated. If flames came, it would be undeniably from God.

Elijah prayed:

**"Answer me, Lord, answer me, so these people will know that you, Lord, are God, and that you are turning their hearts back again."** (1 Kings 18:37, NIV)

## Fire from Heaven

Immediately, fire fell from heaven. It consumed the sacrifice, the wood, the stones, the soil, and even the water in the trench (1 Kings 18:38, NIV). The people fell to the ground and cried out:

**"The Lord—he is God! The Lord—he is God!"** (1 Kings 18:39, NIV)

The undeniable presence of the Lord shattered the silence of Baal. This was more than a victory for Elijah. It was a spiritual awakening for a nation that had wavered too long.

## Lessons from Elijah: Standing Firm in Truth

Elijah's story teaches us that faith is not about numbers but conviction. God answers in His time and in His way. Standing for truth may feel lonely, but it is never in vain.

We face our own "Mount Carmel" moments today, times when cultural pressures us to compromise or remain silent. Elijah's courage reminds us that one voice, aligned with God, can change the course of many.

## Prayer Prompt: Standing in Faith

Bring before God an area in your life where you feel called to take a stand. Ask Him for courage when it feels risky, for conviction when it feels lonely, and for assurance that His power is greater than any opposition.

---

## Community Reflection

- Why do you think God chose fire as the sign on Mount Carmel (1 Kings 18:38–39, NIV)?

- How does Elijah's courage inspire us when we feel outnumbered or isolated?

- What "Mount Carmel" moments might we be facing today—times when we must stand firm in God's truth despite pressure?

---

## Final Reflections: Courage in Conviction

Elijah's stand on Mount Carmel reminds us that courage is not the absence of fear but trust in God's power when the odds seem overwhelming. He faced a king, a queen, and hundreds of prophets, yet he was never truly alone. God was with him, and that was enough.

May we learn to repair our own altars, choose faith over compromise, and trust that God still answers when His people call. Because one person's faith, entirely placed in God, can ignite revival in many.

\*\*\*

## 5.2 Elisha's Miracles: Compassion and Power

Scripture Reference: 2 Kings 2:1–25; 2 Kings 4:1–44; 2 Kings 5:1–27

After the dramatic ministry of Elijah, marked by fire from heaven and bold confrontations with kings, a quieter figure stepped onto the stage. Elisha, Elijah's chosen successor, was not known for thunder and spectacle but for a ministry filled with compassion, provision, and healing. Where Elijah's voice had roared like a storm, Elisha's presence was often like gentle rain—nurturing the poor, comforting families, and reminding Israel that God's care was both powerful and personal.

Elisha's miracles touched every layer of society. Widows found relief in their poverty. Foreigners discovered the mercy of Israel's God. Children experienced resurrection from death—communities shared in miraculous provision. Through him, God revealed that His heart beats especially for the vulnerable, and His power reaches into the ordinary details of life.

$$***$$

## Naaman's Healing: Faith Beyond Borders

Naaman, the commander of the Syrian army, was a man of prestige and power. Yet he carried a hidden shame: leprosy. The disease not only disfigured the body but also caused social and emotional isolation. When Naaman heard of Elisha's reputation, he traveled to Israel in search of healing.

To his surprise, Elisha did not greet him with ceremony or dramatic signs. Instead, a simple message was sent:

**"Go, wash yourself seven times in the Jordan, and your flesh will be restored and you will be cleansed."** (2 Kings 5:10, NIV). The number seven in this context symbolizes completeness and perfection, indicating that Naaman's healing would be thorough and perfect.

Naaman was offended. Surely a prophet would wave his hand, call upon the name of the Lord, and display power. But healing came not through drama but through obedience. When Naaman humbled himself and dipped in the Jordan, his flesh was restored **"like that of a young boy"** (2 Kings 5:14, NIV).

This miracle was more than physical healing. It revealed that God's mercy is not confined to Israel and that true healing requires humility and trust.

## The Widow's Oil: God's Provision in Desperation

Another time, a widow approached Elisha in desperation. Her husband had died, leaving behind debts so outstanding that her children were about to be sold into slavery. Elisha asked her a simple question:

**"Tell me, what do you have in your house?"** (2 Kings 4:2, NIV)

Her answer was heartbreaking: **"Your servant has nothing there at all, except a small jar of olive oil."**

Elisha instructed her to borrow empty jars from her neighbors. As she poured oil into them, the miracle unfolded. Jar after jar filled until none remained empty. The oil stopped flowing only when there were no more vessels left (2 Kings 4:5–6, NIV).

She sold the oil, paid her debts, and saved her children. What little she had, God multiplied. This story echoes across generations: God does not ask us for what we do not have. He blesses what we place in His hands.

***

## Raising the Shunammite's Son: A Miracle of Life

A wealthy Shunammite woman had shown Elisha hospitality, building him a small room to stay whenever he passed through. In gratitude, Elisha promised her a son. Years later, tragedy struck when the boy suddenly collapsed and died in her arms.

The grieving mother refused to give up hope. She traveled to Elisha, clinging to faith that God could restore what was lost. Elisha followed her back, prayed fervently, and stretched himself over the child. Slowly, the boy's body grew warm. He sneezed seven times, and life returned (2 Kings 4:32–35, NIV).

This miracle revealed the heart of God. He is not indifferent to our grief. He enters into it, restoring hope where despair has settled and life where death seems final.

## Feeding a Hundred Men: Provision for the Many

During a time of severe famine, a man brought Elisha twenty loaves of barley bread to share with a hundred hungry men. It was far too little to satisfy them all. But Elisha declared:

**"Give it to the people to eat... They will eat and have some left over."** (2 Kings 4:43, NIV)

And so it was. The bread multiplied. Everyone ate their fill, and food remained (2 Kings 4:44, NIV).

This miracle foreshadowed Jesus' feeding of the five thousand (John 6:1–14, NIV). Both acts remind us that God delights to provide abundantly, turning scarcity into sufficiency and offering a sense of security and reassurance when we place what we have in His hands.

✶✶✶

## The Power of Miracles Today

Elisha's miracles reveal that God's power is never distant or detached. It touches individuals, families, and communities with transformative compassion and purpose, offering hope and inspiration.

Healing comes when pride gives way to humility.

Provision comes when we offer God what little we have.

Restoration comes when grief meets His compassion.

Abundance comes when trust opens the door to His generosity.

Through Elisha's ministry, we glimpse God's heart for His people. He is mighty enough to silence false gods yet tender enough to multiply oil in a widow's home. His miracles whisper to us today that nothing is too small or too significant for His care.

## Prayer Prompt: Trusting in God's Compassion

Bring to God a situation where you need His intervention. It may seem too insignificant to mention or too overwhelming to imagine changing. Ask for faith like Naaman, who obeyed even when it seemed foolish. Ask for trust, as the widow did, by offering her last jar of oil. Ask for perseverance like the Shunammite woman, who refused to stop believing. And ask for openness like the prophets who shared their bread and saw it multiply.

Pray that your eyes may be opened to see God's compassion in both the ordinary and the miraculous.

---

### Community Reflection

- Why do you think Elisha's miracles focused so much on people with low incomes, outsiders, and families?

- How does Naaman's healing show us that God's mercy crosses boundaries?

- What "small jar of oil" do you have that God might want to multiply in your life?

---

## Final Reflections: Compassion and Power

From Elijah's fire on Mount Carmel to Elisha's quiet miracles in homes and fields, we see the complete picture of God's heart. He is both powerful and compassionate, mighty enough to confront false gods and tender enough to rescue a widow from despair. His compassion, a central theme in these stories, is a profound expression of His love and care for His people.

Elisha's miracles remind us that God's power is not abstract or distant. It is personal, meeting us in our weakness, providing for our needs, and pointing us to Christ, the ultimate healer and redeemer.

## 5.3 Isaiah's Vision: Hope and Redemption

Scripture Reference: Isaiah 6:1–13; Isaiah 9:6–7; Isaiah 53:1–12; Isaiah 65:17–25

Isaiah's ministry began during a turbulent period in Israel's history. It was the 8th century BC, a time when the rising power of Assyria threatened the southern kingdom of Judah. Corruption, idolatry, and injustice plagued the people. Kings came and went, but few led with righteousness. Against this backdrop of fear and instability, God raised Isaiah to deliver a message of both judgment and hope.

One defining moment marked the beginning of Isaiah's prophetic call. In a vision, he found himself standing in the temple, surrounded by the sacred stillness of worship. Suddenly, the earthly gave way to the heavenly:

**"I saw the Lord, high and exalted, seated on a throne, and the train of His robe filled the temple."** (Isaiah 6:1, NIV)

Majestic seraphim hovered above, their voices thundering in unceasing praise:

**"Holy, holy, holy is the Lord Almighty; the whole earth is full of His glory."** (Isaiah 6:3, NIV)

The temple shook under the weight of divine majesty. Isaiah was overwhelmed, undone in the presence of God's holiness.

### Isaiah's Transformation

In the brilliance of God's glory, Isaiah saw his own unworthiness:

**"Woe to me! I am ruined! For I am a man of unclean lips, and I live among a people of unclean lips, and my eyes have seen the King, the Lord Almighty."** (Isaiah 6:5, NIV)

But God did not leave him in despair. A seraph took a live coal from the altar and touched Isaiah's lips, saying:

**"Your guilt is taken away and your sin atoned for."** (Isaiah 6:7, NIV)

Purified and forgiven, Isaiah was prepared for his calling. When the Lord asked, **"Whom shall I send? And who will go for us?"**

Isaiah answered with courage: **"Here am I. Send me!"** (Isaiah 6:8, NIV)

This encounter revealed a vital truth: before Isaiah could speak for God, he had to be cleansed by God. His mission was rooted not in his worthiness but in God's grace.

## Prophecies of Redemption and the Coming Savior

Isaiah's message was not only for his own generation but for all time. Though he warned of judgment for sin, he also spoke words of extraordinary hope.

He foretold the birth of a child who would be called the **Prince of Peace**, a ruler whose reign would never end (Isaiah 9:6–7, NIV).

He described a **Suffering Servant**, despised and rejected, pierced for our transgressions, who would bring healing through His wounds (Isaiah 53:5, NIV).

He envisioned a **new heaven and a new earth**, where sorrow and pain would vanish and joy would flourish forever (Isaiah 65:17, NIV).

These prophecies find their ultimate fulfillment in Jesus Christ, the Savior who redeems and restores all who believe.

## Why Isaiah's Vision Still Matters Today

Isaiah's vision continues to speak with timeless relevance. God's holiness reveals our need for transformation.

Redemption is always within reach through His grace. Hope in His promises sustains us through trials.

Just as Isaiah was cleansed and sent, we too are called to encounter God's holiness, receive His forgiveness, and live as witnesses of His hope.

## Living with Hope and Purpose

Isaiah challenges us to ask:

*Are we willing to acknowledge our need for renewal?*

*Will we respond to God's call with the same surrender: "Here am I. Send me"?*

*Do we live each day with the confidence that His promises endure?*

*The vision that transformed Isaiah is meant to transform us as well.*

## Prayer Prompt: Embracing God's Call

Ask God to purify your heart and prepare you for the purpose He has set before you. Pray for the courage to trust His vision for your life, even when the path seems uncertain, and for the boldness to say with Isaiah, "Here am I. Send me."

---

### Community Reflection

- Why do you think Isaiah's vision begins with God's holiness before His call to mission?

- How does Isaiah's encounter mirror our own need for grace before service?

- Which of Isaiah's prophecies about Jesus gives you the most hope today?

---

## Final Reflections: A Vision of Hope

Isaiah's vision reminds us that true mission begins not with our strength but with God's holiness and grace. His prophecies of the Messiah point us to Jesus Christ—the one who redeems, restores, and renews.

May we, like Isaiah, encounter God in His holiness, receive His grace, and answer His call with faith and courage:

**"Here am I. Send me."** (Isaiah 6:8, NIV)

\*\*\*

## 5.4 Jeremiah's Lament: Perseverance in Troubled Times

Scripture Reference: Jeremiah 1:4–10; 20:7–18; 31:31–34; 37:16; 38:6; Lamentations 3:22–23

The story of Jeremiah begins during the last days of Judah's independence, a turbulent period in which Babylon rose to power and threatened Jerusalem. Political alliances were fragile, armies gathered at the borders, and leaders hardened their hearts in rebellion against God. Instead of repentance, idolatry flourished. Into this storm, God called Jeremiah, appointing him as a prophet while he was still a young man (Jeremiah 1:4–10, NIV).

From the beginning, Jeremiah felt the weight of his task. His mission was not to deliver comforting words, but to proclaim warnings of judgment. Imagine standing before kings, priests, and your own neighbors with a message no one wanted to hear. For his faithfulness, Jeremiah was mocked and ridiculed (Jeremiah 20:7, NIV), imprisoned in a dungeon (Jeremiah 37:16, NIV), and even lowered into a cistern to die (Jeremiah 38:6, NIV).

His life was marked by rejection and loneliness, yet he refused to abandon the calling God had placed on him. His courage in the face of such adversity is truly inspiring.

### The Weeping Prophet's Honest Lament

Jeremiah is remembered as the "weeping prophet" because he gave voice to both God's grief and his own. His writings capture raw honesty—anguish, despair, and prayers that wrestle with doubt. In one moment of deep sorrow, he cried out:

**"Cursed be the day I was born! Why did I ever come out of the womb to see trouble and sorrow and to end my days in shame?"** (Jeremiah 20:14, 18, NIV)

These words sound like despair, yet they are also faith. Jeremiah chose to bring his unfiltered pain into God's presence rather than turn away. His laments, a form of prayer that expresses deep sorrow or grief, teach us that God welcomes honesty and meets us even in our darkest prayers.

## A New Covenant: Hope Beyond Exile

Although Jeremiah's message was filled with judgment, it was never without hope. Even as exile loomed, he spoke of a day when God would restore His people through a new covenant:

**"This is the covenant I will make with the people of Israel... I will put my law in their minds and write it on their hearts. I will be their God, and they will be my people."** (Jeremiah 31:33, NIV)

Unlike the old covenant written on stone, this new covenant, a promise of God's grace and forgiveness, would be written on human hearts. It would not depend on ritual sacrifices but on God's forgiveness and renewal, fulfilled in Jesus Christ.

Jeremiah's laments echo through the book of Lamentations, yet even there, hope shines brightly. In the midst of grief, he proclaimed:

**"Because of the Lord's great love we are not consumed, for His compassions never fail. They are new every morning; great is Your faithfulness."** (Lamentations 3:22–23, NIV)

Here is the tension of Jeremiah's life: tears and faith, despair and hope, judgment and redemption.

## Lessons from Jeremiah's Perseverance

Jeremiah's life reveals that faith is not about escaping hardship but enduring it with trust in God. His tears teach us that lament can be an act of faith, not weakness. His prophecies remind us that even when everything seems lost, God's promises stretch beyond our present pain into a future of redemption.

## Holding Onto Hope in Difficult Seasons

We all know what it means to walk through valleys of rejection, loss, or sorrow. Jeremiah shows us that we do not need to hide our struggles from God. We can speak honestly, cry freely, and still cling to hope. Faith does not silence lament. It transforms it into prayer.

## Prayer Prompt: Trusting God Through Trials

If you are in a season of struggle, bring it honestly before God. Ask Him for the endurance to remain faithful, the courage to pray with transparency, and the hope to believe His promises when the future feels uncertain. Remember that His mercies are new every morning, and His faithfulness never fails. Your honest prayers are not a sign of weakness, but a source of strength and support.

---

### Community Reflection

- Why do you think Jeremiah was so open about his pain and discouragement?

- How does his example show that lament can be an act of faith, not weakness?

- What does the "new covenant written on hearts" mean for us today?

---

## Final Reflections on Isaiah and Jeremiah

From Isaiah's breathtaking vision of God's holiness to Jeremiah's weary tears of lament, these prophets reveal two sides of faith. Isaiah's vision reminds us that mission begins with grace: "Here am I. Send me." Jeremiah's perseverance shows us that faith often requires enduring trials with honest faith and trusting that His mercies are new every morning.

Together, their voices proclaim the same truth: **God's *promises never fail*.**

May we hold Isaiah's vision and Jeremiah's perseverance close. Standing in awe of God's glory, enduring trials with honest faith, and trusting that His mercies are new every morning. Because even in our darkest seasons, God is still writing redemption into our story.

***

## 5.5 Jonah's Reluctance: Obedience and Mercy

Scripture Reference: Jonah 1:1–4:11

The book of Jonah begins not with a gentle invitation but with a startling command. God tells Jonah to go to Nineveh, the capital of Assyria, a city infamous for cruelty, violence, and oppression. To Israel, Assyria was not only an enemy but a terror. For Jonah, the idea of preaching there was unthinkable.

**"Go to the great city of Nineveh and preach against it, because its wickedness has come up before me."** (Jonah 1:2, NIV)

Instead of obeying, Jonah runs in the opposite direction. He boards a ship to Tarshish, likely the farthest known place westward. This wasn't simply a matter of distance; it was outright defiance. Jonah wasn't afraid of failure; he was scared of success. He didn't want Nineveh to repent. He didn't want God's mercy to extend to Israel's enemies.

### A Storm, a Fish, and a Second Chance

As Jonah flees, God sends a violent storm. The ship threatens to break apart. The sailors, desperate, cast lots and discover Jonah is the cause. He admits:

**"I know that it is my fault that this great storm has come upon you."** (Jonah 1:12, NIV)

At Jonah's urging, the sailors reluctantly throw him into the sea. Immediately, the storm ceases. In an ironic twist, the pagan sailors begin to worship the Lord while Jonah sinks into the deep.

But God is not finished with him. A great fish swallows Jonah, and for three days and nights, he dwells in darkness. Inside the fish, Jonah prays, confessing his helplessness and acknowledging God's deliverance (Jonah 2:1–10, NIV). After this prayer, the fish spits him onto dry land. Jonah receives what few ever do: a second chance to obey.

Jesus Himself later pointed to this moment as a foreshadowing of His own mission:

**"For as Jonah was three days and three nights in the belly of a huge fish, so the Son of Man will be three days and three nights in the heart of the earth."** (Matthew 12:40, NIV)

Jonah's confinement in the fish was not only his personal rescue—it became a symbol of Christ's death, burial, and resurrection, the ultimate act of mercy for all humanity.

## Nineveh's Repentance and God's Mercy

This time, Jonah goes. His message is brief and without passion:

**"Forty more days and Nineveh will be overthrown."** (Jonah 3:4, NIV)

Yet the people of Nineveh respond with astonishing humility. From the king to the commoner, they fast, repent, and turn from evil. Even their animals are covered in sackcloth as a sign of collective grief and repentance. Seeing their change of heart, God shows mercy and spares the city.

Jonah, however, is outraged. He confesses the real reason he fled in the first place:

**"Isn't this what I said, Lord, when I was still at home? That is why I tried to forestall by fleeing to Tarshish. I knew that you are a gracious and compassionate God, slow to anger and abounding in love."** (Jonah 4:2, NIV)

Jonah wanted justice. God gave mercy.

## A Lesson in Compassion

Still sulking, Jonah sits outside the city, waiting to see if perhaps God will destroy it after all. God provides a leafy plant to shade him from the sun, then sends a worm to wither it. Jonah laments the loss of the plant, revealing that he cared more about his temporary comfort than about the fate of thousands.

God responds with a lesson that closes the book:

**"You have been concerned about this plant, though you did not tend it or make it grow... And should I not have concern for the great city of Nineveh, in which there are more than 120,000 people?"** (Jonah 4:10–11, NIV)

The contrast is clear: Jonah's narrow compassion versus God's expansive mercy.

## Lessons from Jonah's Life

Jonah's story is not just about a runaway prophet. It is about the character of God.

God's mercy is greater than our prejudices.

Obedience is not based on our comfort but on God's command.

Redemption belongs to God alone—He chooses whom to save.

Jonah challenges us to examine our own hearts. Do we resist God's calling because it pushes us beyond our preferences? Do we secretly hold back mercy from those we dislike? Jonah reminds us that God's compassion will always exceed our limits.

## Prayer Prompt: Accepting God's Mercy

Ask God to reveal any prejudices or reluctance that keep you from embracing His call. Pray for a heart softened toward those you find challenging to love. Thank Him for the mercy He has shown you, and ask for courage to extend that same mercy to others.

## Community Reflection

- Why do you think Jonah resisted preaching to Nineveh so strongly?

- What does this story reveal about God's heart for even our enemies?

- How do Jonah's three days in the fish foreshadow Christ's death and resurrection?

## Final Reflections: Mercy That Surprises Us

Jonah's story is not about a prophet swallowed by a fish but about a God whose mercy swallows up even the darkest sin. It reminds us that His compassion extends to outsiders, enemies, and even the reluctant messenger himself.

We may run, hesitate, or resist, but God's purposes prevail. And when His mercy surprises us, it calls us to rejoice, not resent. For His heart is always for redemption—both ours and the redemption of those we least expect.

## 5.6 Daniel in the Lion's Den: Faithfulness Under Pressure

Scripture Reference: Daniel 6:1–28

Daniel's story is one of the most beloved in Scripture, not just because of the dramatic rescue from lions, but because it shows us what faithfulness looks like over an entire lifetime. By this point in the narrative, Daniel was no longer a young exile in Babylon. He was likely in his 80s, a man who had served under multiple kings and empires with remarkable integrity.

Even in a foreign land, surrounded by pagan rulers and constant political intrigue, Daniel's reputation was spotless. His consistency made him trustworthy to kings but also stirred deep jealousy among other officials. They could find no corruption or negligence in his leadership, so they looked for another way to destroy him.

They knew Daniel's true allegiance lay with his God.

### A Trap of Loyalty

The jealous officials convinced King Darius to issue a decree:

**"Anyone who prays to any god or human being during the next thirty days, except to you, Your Majesty, shall be thrown into the lion's den."** (Daniel 6:7, NIV)

It was a law designed for one man only—Daniel. They knew he prayed faithfully three times a day, every day, no matter the circumstance.

When Daniel learned of the decree, he did not hide or compromise. He went home, opened his windows toward Jerusalem, and prayed as he always had:

**"Three times a day he got down on his knees and prayed, giving thanks to his God, just as he had done before."** (Daniel 6:10, NIV)

His obedience wasn't an act of rebellion or panic. It was simply the rhythm of his devotion, practiced for a lifetime.

## Thrown to the Lions

The officials wasted no time. They reported Daniel's prayers, forcing King Darius to carry out the law of the Medes and Persians, which could not be revoked. Though the king respected Daniel, he had no choice but to condemn him.

Daniel was thrown into the den of lions, a real execution pit meant to end life swiftly and violently. Yet Daniel's trust in God never wavered.

That night, God sent an angel to shut the mouths of the lions. Daniel was kept safe in the very place designed for his destruction.

At dawn, the anxious king rushed to the pit and cried out:

**"Daniel, servant of the living God, has your God, whom you serve continually, been able to rescue you from the lions?"** (Daniel 6:20, NIV)

To his joy, a voice responded:

**"My God sent His angel, and He shut the mouths of the lions. They have not hurt me."** (Daniel 6:22, NIV)

Daniel was lifted out unharmed, a living testimony that God's protection is greater than any earthly threat.

## A King's Decree and God's Glory

Overwhelmed by the miracle, King Darius issued a new decree, declaring the greatness of Israel's God:

**"For He is the living God and He endures forever; His kingdom will not be destroyed, His dominion will never end."** (Daniel 6:26, NIV)

Through Daniel's unwavering faith, an entire empire was confronted with the truth of God's power and sovereignty.

## Lessons from Daniel: Faith Under Fire

Daniel's life offers enduring lessons for us today:

Faithfulness means staying steady in prayer and obedience, even when the cost is high.

God's protection is not always about removing us from trials, but about sustaining us within them.

One person's consistency can inspire many and even bring glory to God among those who do not yet believe.

**Daniel challenges us to ask:**

*Are we willing to remain faithful when our convictions are tested?*

*Do we trust God's deliverance, even when surrounded by our own "lions"?*

*How does the daily rhythm of prayer prepare us for life's greatest trials?*

## Prayer Prompt: Strength in Trials

Ask God to give you courage to remain faithful in moments of testing. Pray for boldness to live out your faith consistently, and for strength to trust Him when circumstances seem overwhelming.

---

### Community Reflection

- Why was Daniel's habit of prayer so central to his survival in this story?

- How does his faith at age 80+ challenge our own view of lifelong perseverance?

- What "lion's dens" might believers face today, and how can we support each other in those trials?

---

## Final Reflections on Jonah and Daniel

From Jonah's reluctance to Daniel's unwavering faith, we see two contrasting responses to God's call. Jonah resisted, running in defiance.

Daniel remained steadfast, praying in devotion even when death loomed. Both stories remind us of timeless truths:

God's mercy extends further than our prejudices or preferences.

Obedience is not about convenience but about trust.

Faithfulness in adversity glorifies God and inspires others.

As we face challenges of our own, may we remember Jonah's lesson to extend mercy beyond ourselves, and Daniel's witness to stand firm even when surrounded by lions. In every act of obedience and every trial endured, God proves Himself faithful.

# Chapter 6

# The Teachings of Jesus

I remember the first time the Sermon on the Mount truly gripped my heart. It was a quiet morning, the world outside still waking up. I sat in my favorite armchair, a steaming cup of tea in hand, flipping through the pages of Matthew 5–7.

What I read that day turned my understanding of success and fulfillment upside down.

Jesus was not offering a path to earthly achievement. He was revealing a way of life that defied the values of the world. He declared that the poor in spirit were blessed, that the meek would inherit the earth, and that those who mourn would find comfort. These were not just poetic words; they were a radical vision for living in

alignment with God's heart.

As I read, I could almost imagine the scene—men, women, and children gathered on a hillside, the early morning breeze carrying the smell of fresh grass, the hum of anticipation filling the air. Some came out of curiosity, while others were driven by desperation. Many had wounds of poverty, grief, or oppression under Roman rule. All of them longed for hope. And in the middle of their yearning, Jesus began to speak words that turned the world upside down.

## 6.1 The Sermon on the Mount: Radical Love and Kingdom Values

Scripture Reference: Matthew 5:1–7:29

The sun rose gently over the hills of Galilee, spilling golden light across a crowd that had gathered with expectation. Farmers weary from toil, mothers clutching children, young zealots dreaming of freedom, and elders carrying stories of God's promises—all stood together, waiting. Each person carried questions, doubts, and hopes, and all eyes turned to Jesus as He made His way to the top of the hill.

When He sat down, silence swept across the multitude. Rabbis always taught from a seated posture, the recognized position of authority. The people leaned forward, hungry for words of life. And then Jesus began—not with commands, not with threats, but with blessings.

**"Blessed are the poor in spirit... Blessed are those who mourn... Blessed are the meek."** (Matthew 5:1–12, NIV)

It was unlike anything they had heard before. In a world where Rome celebrated power, wealth, and conquest, Jesus declared that God's favor rested on the humble, the grieving, and the merciful. His words were not just comfort for the brokenhearted; they were a radical redefinition of what it meant to live under God's rule.

This was not a political manifesto or a call to revolution. It was an invitation into a Kingdom unlike any other; a Kingdom where greatness was found in humility, strength in gentleness, and life in surrender.

### More Than Rules—A Transformed Heart

Many came expecting Jesus to teach a new set of rules, but He gave them something more profound. He went beyond outward behavior to the very heart of human motives.

**"You have heard that it was said, 'Love your neighbor and hate your enemy.' But I tell you, love your enemies and pray for those who persecute you."** (Matthew 5:43–44, NIV)

Jesus was not concerned with outward obedience alone. He was calling for inner renewal. Forgiveness was not weakness. It was strength that broke the chains of resentment. Mercy was not passivity. It was courage to extend grace where none was expected. Holiness was not about keeping appearances. It was about being transformed from the inside out.

This call to radical love and peacemaking was (and still is) one of the most difficult and countercultural aspects of Jesus' teaching. And yet, it is also the most life-changing.

## Living the Sermon on the Mount

The words of Jesus were never meant to be admired from a distance. They were meant to be lived in the grit of daily life. How do we respond when someone wrongs us? Do we cling to pride, or do we embrace humility? Are we willing to love those who oppose us?

Though challenging, these teachings remain transformative. They open the way to inner peace, restored relationships, and a deeper communion with God.

## A Call to Radical Love

As you reflect on Jesus' teaching, consider:

*Who in your life do you struggle to forgive?*

*Where can you choose peace instead of conflict?*

*How can you embody mercy in your daily interactions?*

## Prayer Prompt: Walking in Radical Love

Bring before God someone you find difficult to love or forgive. Be honest about your feelings, and ask Him to help you see them through His eyes. Pray for the strength to love even when it is hard. Ask for grace to replace bitterness, courage to pursue peace, and wisdom to take even small steps of kindness that reflect Christ's love.

**Community Reflection**

- How does Jesus' definition of "blessing" in the Beatitudes challenge the world's idea of success?

- What examples have you seen of forgiveness or mercy that transformed a relationship or situation?

- In your community, what would it look like to live out Jesus' call to be peacemakers?

## Final Reflections: The Challenge and Beauty of Jesus' Teachings

The Sermon on the Mount is not a list of ideals—it is a revolutionary way of life.

It calls us to love when the world says hate, to forgive when the world seeks revenge, to pursue humility when the world demands power. It challenges us to release pride and fear, embracing instead a life of grace, mercy, and love.

As we seek to follow Jesus, may we not only admire His words but also embody them in the way we live, love, and serve.

## Living the Sermon on the Mount Today

Forgive when the world says hold a grudge.

Choose humility over self-promotion.

Love your enemies, not only your friends.

Break cycles of bitterness with mercy.

Allow your heart to be transformed, not just your behavior.

## 6.2 The Parable of the Good Samaritan: Compassion Beyond Boundaries

Scripture Reference: Luke 10:25–37

It began with a question that seemed ordinary but carried immense weight. A lawyer, respected for his knowledge of the Law, stood up to test Jesus. The crowd leaned in, sensing the challenge. This was not an innocent inquiry but a calculated attempt to trap a teacher whose words often overturned expectations.

**"Teacher, what must I do to inherit eternal life?"** (Luke 10:25, NIV)

Rather than answering directly, Jesus turned the question back:

**"What is written in the Law? How do you read it?"**

The man replied with confidence, quoting what every faithful Jew knew by heart:

**"Love the Lord your God with all your heart and with all your soul and with all your strength and with all your mind, and love your neighbor as yourself."** (Luke 10:27, NIV)

**"You have answered correctly,"** Jesus said. **"Do this and you will live."** (Luke 10:28, NIV)

But the man, unwilling to leave the matter there, pressed further. Perhaps hoping to justify his own prejudices, he asked, **"And who is my neighbor?"** (Luke 10:29, NIV).

The question cut to the core of the human heart. It was not about definitions but about limits. How far must love extend? Who counts as "neighbor"? With that, Jesus told a story that would dismantle assumptions and forever redefine compassion.

### A Shocking Twist in the Story

A man was traveling the dangerous road from Jerusalem to Jericho when robbers attacked him. Beaten, stripped, and left half dead, he lay helpless on the roadside (Luke 10:30, NIV).

A priest came by. Surely this man of God would stop. But he crossed to the other side and kept walking.

Then came a Levite, another highly regarded religious figure. He too saw the man, but he also passed by.

Finally, a Samaritan appeared. To the Jewish audience, this was unthinkable. Centuries of animosity divided Jews and Samaritans. They viewed each other with suspicion and contempt. Yet it was this outsider, the one least expected, who stopped, inspiring us with his unexpected heroism.

He approached the wounded man with compassion, tending his wounds with oil and wine, placing him on his own donkey, and bringing him to an inn. There he paid the innkeeper two denarii, enough for several weeks of care, and promised to cover any additional costs (Luke 10:33–35, NIV).

The hero of the story was not the priest or the Levite but the Samaritan. His compassion crossed cultural boundaries, and his mercy defied prejudice.

## Breaking Down Barriers to Love

Jesus could have chosen any character as the hero, but He deliberately chose a Samaritan. In doing so, He shattered the boundaries of who could be called **"neighbor."**

The priest and Levite had status and knowledge of the Law, but they lacked compassion. The Samaritan, though despised by the Jews, revealed what true love looks like: costly, inconvenient, and rooted in mercy.

Jesus ended with a piercing question:

**"Which of these three do you think was a neighbor to the man who fell into the hands of robbers?"** (Luke 10:36, NIV)

The lawyer could not bring himself to say "the Samaritan." Instead, he answered, **"The one who had mercy on him."** (Luke 10:37, NIV)

And Jesus said, **"Go and do likewise."**

## Living Out the Good Samaritan's Compassion

This parable is not only about helping strangers. It challenges us to confront our prejudices, break down barriers, and extend compassion even when it is uncomfortable. It's a reminder that compassion has the power to transform, giving us hope and encouragement.

Consider these moments in our own world.

A commuter stops to help a stranger whose car has broken down on a busy highway, even though they are late for work.

A family opens their home to refugees from a culture and language very different from their own, choosing welcome over fear.

A young person speaks up against bullying in their school, standing beside the student who is most often ignored or ridiculed.

These acts may seem ordinary, but they carry extraordinary weight. They reflect the heart of the Good Samaritan. This love chooses action over excuse, mercy over prejudice, and compassion over convenience.

The call is clear: to love expansively, inclusively, and sacrificially, just as Jesus modeled.

## Prayer Prompt: Becoming a Neighbor

Ask God to open your eyes to the needs around you and to give you courage to act. Pray for the grace to love those who are difficult to love, the humility to cross barriers, and the willingness to reflect His mercy in practical ways. Pray for specific situations where you can show compassion and love to those in need.

## Community Reflection

- What boundaries, whether cultural, social, or personal, might keep us from seeing someone as our "neighbor"?

- How can the church today embody the radical inclusivity Jesus taught in this parable?

- When have you experienced compassion from an unexpected person, and how did it shape your understanding of love?

## Final Reflections: Love Without Limits

The parable of the Good Samaritan is more than a story. It is a summons to live differently. Love does not stop at comfort zones or cultural lines. It does not ask who deserves help. True love acts, regardless of convenience or prejudice. This message empowers us and motivates us to love without limits.

As we reflect on this parable, we should remember that our neighbor is anyone in need, no matter their background or status. And may we choose to love with a compassion that mirrors Christ's: selfless, boundary-breaking, and filled with grace.

## Living the Good Samaritan Today

See interruptions as opportunities to show love.

Remember that compassion is greater than convenience.

Refuse to let prejudice dictate your actions.

Be a neighbor to those who cannot repay you.

Trust that even small acts of mercy reflect the heart of God.

## 6.3 The Prodigal Son: Grace and Reconciliation

Scripture Reference: Luke 15:11–32

Jesus often told stories that pierced through cultural expectations and personal defenses. These stories revealed the shocking depth of God's love. Among them, the parable of the Prodigal Son stands as one of the most moving and profound.

Picture the scene: religious leaders and ordinary people alike had gathered around Him. Tax collectors and sinners drew close to hear His words. At the same time, Pharisees and teachers of the law muttered in disapproval, saying, **"This man welcomes sinners and eats with them"** (Luke 15:2, NIV). It was in this setting that Jesus told a story designed to shatter their assumptions about who deserves love and who receives grace.

**"There was a man who had two sons."** (Luke 15:11, NIV)

Immediately, the listeners leaned in. Families were central to Jewish life, and inheritance was sacred. What followed would have stunned His audience.

## A Son's Rebellion

The younger son grew restless, weary of routine, and impatient for independence. He wanted freedom without responsibility, riches without relationship. His demand was shocking:

**"Father, give me my share of the inheritance."** (Luke 15:12, NIV)

Such a request was as reasonable as wishing his father dead. Yet, in a twist that defied cultural norms, the father granted it. He divided his property, surrendering what represented years of sacrifice and care.

The son gathered his wealth, left home, and squandered everything on reckless living. His pursuit of pleasure soon turned to despair when famine struck. Hungry and humiliated, he ended up feeding pigs—an unthinkable job for a Jew—longing for scraps of food.

At last, in his desperation, he rehearsed a confession. Maybe his father would take him back as a servant.

## An Extravagant Welcome

While he was still far off, the father saw him. Compassion welled up within him. In an act unthinkable for a dignified elder of the community, he ran to his son, embraced him, and kissed him (Luke 15:20, NIV).

Before the son could finish his prepared apology, the father restored him fully.

A robe was placed on him, covering his shame.

A ring was given, restoring his authority as a son.

A feast was prepared, declaring joy over his return.

**"For this son of mine was dead and is alive again; he was lost and is found."** (Luke 15:24, NIV)

It was not a lecture, nor probation, but pure grace.

## The Elder Brother's Resentment

But grace did not sit easily with everyone. The older brother, who had labored faithfully, heard the music and celebration. Anger burned within him.

**"All these years I've been slaving for you and never disobeyed your orders. Yet you never gave me even a young goat so I could celebrate with my friends."** (Luke 15:29, NIV)

His resentment exposed another form of lostness. Though he remained physically close, his heart was far away. He could not rejoice at his brother's return because bitterness blinded him.

The father, gentle and patient, reminded him:

**"My son, you are always with me, and everything I have is yours."** (Luke 15:31, NIV)

Both sons had been lost—the younger in rebellion, the elder in self-righteousness. And the father loved them both.

## The Call to Grace

This parable reveals the radical heart of God. His love defies human expectations. His grace embraces both the wayward and the self-righteous.

Perhaps you see yourself in the prodigal, returning home after failures and mistakes, longing for mercy. Or maybe you see yourself in the elder brother, struggling to extend grace to others, resentful when God's love seems too generous.

Wherever you find yourself, the Father's invitation is the same: come home, rejoice, and share in His joy.

---

### Community Reflection

- Which son do you most identify with in this season of your life—the prodigal or the elder brother?

- How can our communities learn to celebrate grace rather than withhold it when someone returns or repents?

- What does this parable teach us about the Father's heart, and how can we reflect that same grace in our own relationships?

---

## Prayer Prompt: Embracing Grace

Bring to God the relationships where grace feels hardest to extend or receive. Ask Him to heal the wounds that fuel resentment and soften your heart with His mercy. Pray for the humility to accept His grace for yourself and the courage to extend it freely to others.

## Final Reflections: The Power of Jesus' Parables

The parable of the Prodigal Son is not merely about a family; it is about the Gospel itself. It shows us that:

Love is not earned—it is given.

Grace is not measured—it is lavish.

Forgiveness is not fair—it is divine.

From the Good Samaritan's radical compassion to the father's extravagant welcome, Jesus' parables reveal a God whose mercy knows no limits.

May we step into that mercy, forgive beyond fairness, and rejoice whenever the lost are found. Because grace is not just a story—it is the heart of God.

***

## 6.4 The Beatitudes: The Heart of Jesus' Message

*Scripture Reference: Matthew 5:1–12*

At the opening of the Sermon on the Mount, a significant event in Jesus' ministry where He delivered many of His key teachings, Jesus offered a series of blessings that have come to be known as the Beatitudes. These words laid out the values of His Kingdom in contrast to the values of the world.

**"Blessed are those who hunger and thirst for righteousness, for they will be filled. Blessed are the merciful, for they will be shown mercy. Blessed are the pure in heart, for they will see God. Blessed are the peacemakers, for they will be called children of God."** (Matthew 5:6–9, NIV)

These blessings show us that God's favor rests not on the powerful or influential but on those who long for justice, who live with integrity, who extend mercy, and who bring peace into a fractured world. Each Beatitude reframes what it means to be truly blessed, shifting our focus from temporary success to the assurance of eternal reward, instilling in us a sense of confidence and reassurance in our faith.

The Beatitudes are not mere lofty ideals to be admired from a distance. They are powerful invitations to live a transformed life. They remind us that in God's Kingdom, humility leads to greatness, mercy triumphs over judgment, and those who suffer for righteousness are honored in heaven. This transformative power should inspire and give hope to our spiritual growth.

## A Radical Reversal of Values

Each Beatitude presents a way of life that stands in stark contrast to the world's values.

Those who recognize their deep need for God are promised the Kingdom. Those who mourn the weight of brokenness will be comforted. The meek, who choose strength clothed in gentleness, will inherit the earth.

Society rarely celebrates such qualities, yet Jesus places them at the very center of His Kingdom. The Beatitudes turn the value system of the world upside down, reminding us that God blesses what people often dismiss. This countercultural nature of the Beatitudes challenges us to live differently and be a light in the world.

## Transforming the Individual and the Community

The Beatitudes are not just about personal spirituality. They form the blueprint for a community that reflects God's heart. They invite us to embrace humility instead of pride, mercy instead of judgment, and perseverance even in the face of persecution. This communal aspect of the Beatitudes makes us feel connected and part of a larger purpose.

When lived out, these virtues create a culture of peace and grace. They shape relationships, strengthen communities, and make the people of God a living witness to His Kingdom on earth.

## Embodying the Beatitudes in Daily Life

The Beatitudes are not abstract ideals to admire from afar. They are invitations to live differently.

*Where can you cultivate greater humility in your daily interactions?*

*How can you bring comfort to those who mourn?*

*What opportunities do you have to pursue peace, even when it is costly?*

Jesus calls us not just to hear these words, but to embody them. They are the heartbeat of Kingdom living, transforming us from the inside out.

---

### Community Reflection

- Which Beatitude feels most challenging for you to live out, and why?

- How would a community shaped by these values look different from the world around it?

- What practical steps could your church, family, or small group take to embody the Beatitudes together?

---

## Prayer Prompt: Living the Beatitudes

Ask God to help you embody these virtues in your daily life. Pray for wisdom in your decisions, compassion in your relationships, and courage to live with integrity even when it is difficult. Ask Him to form in you a heart that seeks His blessing rather than the applause of the world. Specifically, you can pray for the strength to be meek in a world that values power, or for the grace to be merciful when it's easier to hold onto grudges. These prayers can help align your heart with the values of God's Kingdom.

## Final Reflections: The Upside-Down Kingdom

The Beatitudes remind us that God's Kingdom, often referred to in the Bible as the reign of God's love and justice, is not built on power, wealth, or status. It is built on humility, mercy, purity, and peace. This is a Kingdom where those who suffer are comforted, where the overlooked are honored, and where love triumphs over pride. Understanding and embracing this Kingdom is key to living out the Beatitudes in our daily lives.

As you reflect on Jesus' words, embrace the upside-down Kingdom. True blessing is not found in worldly success but in living aligned with God's presence and favor.

## Living the Beatitudes Today

**Blessed are the poor in spirit** - Depend entirely on God, not on yourself.

**Blessed are those who mourn -** Bring your grief to Him; He is near to the brokenhearted.

**Blessed are the meek** - Choose gentleness and humility over pride and control.

**Blessed are those who hunger and thirst for righteousness** - Desire God's ways more than worldly success.

**Blessed are the merciful** - Offer forgiveness freely, just as you have been forgiven.

**Blessed are the pure in heart** - Keep your motives pure, seeking God above all else.

**Blessed are the peacemakers -** Build bridges of reconciliation rather than walls of division.

**Blessed are those persecuted for righteousness** - Stand firm in faith, knowing God honors your endurance.

## 6.5 The Rich Young Ruler: Prioritizing Eternal Treasures

Scripture Reference: Matthew 19:16–22; Mark 10:17–22; Luke 18:18–23

Picture the moment: a wealthy young man, dressed in fine robes, pushes through the crowd and kneels before Jesus. His posture shows eagerness, even humility, but his eyes reveal a deeper question—one that success and riches have not answered.

**"Teacher, what good thing must I do to inherit eternal life?"** (Matthew 19:16, NIV)

It was a noble question, but it carried a subtle assumption: that eternal life could be earned through human effort. On the surface, his life seemed flawless. He had kept the commandments, honored tradition, and lived with moral integrity. Yet beneath the polished exterior, something was missing. Despite his wealth and respect, his soul still ached for assurance.

Jesus acknowledged his devotion but then spoke words that pierced directly to the heart:

**"Go, sell your possessions and give to the poor, and you will have treasure in heaven. Then come, follow me."** (Matthew 19:21, NIV)

The challenge was clear. Eternal life was not about doing more but about surrender—releasing what bound him and embracing discipleship. For a moment, perhaps hope flickered. Could it be this simple? Yet the weight of wealth, identity, and pride proved too heavy. With sorrow in his eyes, he turned and walked away.

## The Struggle Between Comfort and Calling

This story is not only about money but about where our hearts find security. The young man's riches weren't just possessions; they defined his worth, his comfort, and his identity. To let them go felt like losing himself.

Mark's account adds a tender detail: **"Jesus looked at him and loved him."** (Mark 10:21, NIV).

The invitation was not harsh but compassionate. Jesus was not trying to rob him of joy but to free him from chains he could not see. The promise of treasure in heaven was greater than anything he would leave behind—yet he could not release his grip.

## A Challenge for Us Today

Most of us are not defined by immense wealth, but we all have things that compete for our devotion. For some, it is comfort and security. For others, it is success, recognition, or material attachments that distract us from deeper obedience.

The rich young ruler's struggle is our struggle. Jesus' invitation still stands: let go, not to lose, but to gain. Eternal treasure cannot be bought or earned. It is received by those who release what hinders them and follow Him fully.

## Reflecting on Our Attachments

What are the things in your life that may be holding you back from fully following Jesus?

Where might God be calling you to prioritize eternal treasures over temporary ones?

How can generosity and simplicity reshape your faith and your view of success?

---

## Community Reflection

- Why do you think the rich young ruler struggled to let go, even when eternal treasure was promised?

- What "comfort zones" keep faith communities from radical obedience today?

- How can we encourage one another to live generously, releasing what competes with God in our lives?

## Prayer Prompt: Releasing What Holds Us Back

Ask God to reveal the areas in your life that compete for your heart. Pray for courage to surrender security, status, or possessions that keep you from following Him fully. Thank Him for the freedom and joy that come from valuing eternal treasure above all else.

## Final Reflections: Choosing Treasure that Lasts

The rich young ruler walked away sad, not because Jesus demanded too much, but because he clung to too little. His wealth could not buy eternal life, and his comfort could not satisfy the longing of his soul.

True wealth is found not in possessions but in God's presence. Eternal treasure belongs to those who release what binds them and embrace the life of discipleship.

### As we reflect on his story, may we:

Release what holds us back.

Choose faith over comfort.

Trust that God's promises outweigh temporary gain.

Because in the end, treasure in heaven never fades, and following Jesus is always worth the cost.

## Living Eternal Treasure Today

Choose generosity over accumulation.

Find identity in Christ, not in possessions.

Practice small daily acts of surrender.

Encourage others to value eternal rewards over temporary gains.

***

## 6.6 The Bread of Life: Satisfying the Soul's Deepest Hunger

*Scripture Reference: John 6:1–71*

Imagine a hillside alive with movement, families gathered, children running between the crowds, the air filled with murmurs of expectation. The people had followed Jesus out of the towns, drawn by His teaching and the hope of healing, but soon their stomachs growled with hunger. What began as wonder now threatened to turn into restlessness.

Then came the miracle. With only five loaves and two fish, Jesus gave thanks, broke the bread, and passed it to the disciples. Basket after basket was carried through the crowd, and to everyone's amazement, it never ran out (Matthew 14:17–21, NIV). Men, women, and children ate until they were full, leaving scraps of bread behind.

That night, as families settled down under the stars, their hunger had been satisfied, but more than their bellies were full. Their hearts burned with the thought: Who is this man that even the impossible bends to His will?

By morning, the crowd sought Him again. They were not ready to let go of the one who could multiply bread and fish. But when they found Him, Jesus did not perform another miracle. Instead, He spoke words that pierced beneath the surface of their desire:

**"Do not work for food that spoils, but for food that endures to eternal life."** (John 6:27, NIV)

In that moment, He shifted their focus. They had come looking for bread to fill their stomachs. He offered bread to fill their souls.

### More Than Physical Sustenance

Jesus knew their hunger went deeper than bread. He declared:

**"I am the Bread of Life. Whoever comes to me will never go hungry."** (John 6:35, NIV)

He was not offering mere physical provision. He was offering Himself as the source of true fulfillment, nourishment that goes beyond survival to eternal life. But many struggled with this teaching. When He spoke of eating His flesh and drinking His blood, His words sounded offensive and incomprehensible. They wanted miracles and signs, not surrender and dependence.

As John records, **"On hearing it, many of his disciples said, 'This is a hard teaching. Who can accept it?'... From this time many of his disciples turned back and no longer followed him."** (John 6:60, 66, NIV)

The crowd that had feasted on bread walked away, unwilling to embrace the Bread of Life. Following Jesus was not just about receiving gifts. It required total trust in Him.

## Feeding the Soul, Not Just the Body

We, too, often chase temporary satisfaction.

We pursue success, relationships, or comfort, yet still feel empty.

We cling to possessions and security, yet remain restless.

We hunger for meaning, but look for it in things that cannot satisfy.

Jesus offers something far greater. He calls us to a life sustained by faith, nourished by His presence, and filled by His Spirit. The Bread of Life is not a quick fix. It is a daily dependence, a relationship that sustains through every season of life.

## Developing Spiritual Hunger

Spiritual growth requires nourishment, just as our bodies do. We must ask ourselves:

Are we feeding our souls with what truly satisfies?

Do we take time to sit in God's presence?

Are we seeking fulfillment in Him rather than in temporary things?

True satisfaction does not come from chasing what fades. It comes from the One who never changes.

---

### Community Reflection

- Why do you think many walked away when Jesus revealed Himself as the Bread of Life?

- In what ways do we, even as believers, sometimes prefer "bread that spoils" over eternal nourishment?

- How can our families, churches, or small groups help one another develop a deeper hunger for God's Word and presence?

- What does it mean today to "stay with Jesus" when His teachings feel difficult or countercultural?

---

It's in these communities that we find support, encouragement, and shared experiences that can deepen our hunger for God. Together, we can foster a hunger for God's Word and presence that sustains us through every season of life.

## Prayer Prompt: Feeding Your Soul

Ask God to give you a hunger for Him that outweighs every other craving. Pray for the desire to seek Him daily, to find nourishment in His Word, and to be sustained by His presence in both joy and hardship.

## Final Thoughts: The Challenge of Jesus' Teachings

The Bread of Life discourse reminds us that following Jesus is not about temporary satisfaction. It is about complete dependence on Him as the trustworthy source of life. Just as bread sustains the body, Christ sustains the soul. Many turned away because the cost of surrender felt too high, but those who stayed discovered a faith that could not be shaken.

From the Beatitudes to the call of discipleship, from the hunger for God to the surrender of earthly attachments, Jesus' teachings show us a path that is radical and deeply fulfilling. They challenge us to redefine what it means to be blessed, to let go of temporary things for eternal treasures, and to find true contentment in Him.

**As we continue our journey, may we:**

Live out the values of the Beatitudes.

Release the things that keep us from following Jesus fully.

May we find our deepest satisfaction in the Bread of Life, Jesus Christ. In Him, we discover not just daily bread, but eternal life and everything our souls truly need. He is the ultimate source of satisfaction, the one who can fill our deepest hunger and bring us true contentment.

Because in Him, we discover not just daily bread, but eternal life and everything our souls truly need.

# Chapter 7

# Acts and Apostolic Letters

I remember the first time I found myself in a gathering of passionate believers. It was not in a cathedral with stained-glass windows or in a stadium filled with thousands, but in a simple church basement. Folding chairs were arranged in uneven rows, the hum of a coffee maker filled the background, and the air carried a sense of unity and belonging. We weren't just meeting to talk about life; we were searching for something more profound, and we found it in each other.

As we prayed and sang, I felt something stir inside me, a unity that bound us together as though we were part of something far greater. It was not about the room or the program. It was about God's presence.

That memory takes me back to another gathering described in Scripture, the day of Pentecost. A group of Jesus' followers were huddled together in an upper room, uncertain of what was next, waiting on the promise Jesus had given them. In that moment of waiting, everything changed.

***

## 7.1 Pentecost: The Birth of the Church

Scripture Reference: Acts 2:1–41

Imagine being in that upper room. The disciples were not in a position of power or privilege. They were ordinary men and women who had seen their Teacher crucified and resurrected. Now they were waiting, just as He had instructed them, but they had no idea what form His promise would take. Hearts pounded. Whispers filled the silence. Every creak of the house must have sharpened their anticipation.

And suddenly it happened.

A sound like a violent rushing wind filled the room. It wasn't a soft breeze; it roared with power, shaking the very walls. Then something even stranger: what looked like tongues of fire appeared and rested on each of them. Fire in the Bible often symbolizes God's presence, and here it was not destroying but empowering. Each disciple was marked, filled with the Holy Spirit. This was a moment of transformation, a sign of the power of the Spirit to change ordinary lives into extraordinary vessels of God's love. (Acts 2:1–4, NIV)

This was no private experience. They began to speak in other languages, declaring the wonders of God. Crowds from every nation who had gathered in Jerusalem for the Feast of Weeks—known as Pentecost—were stunned to hear God's message in their own tongue.

For those unfamiliar with Pentecost, it was a Jewish festival, fifty days after Passover, celebrating the wheat harvest and the giving of the Law at Sinai. On this very day, God chose to give something even greater—the gift of His Spirit. Instead of the Law written on stone, His Spirit would now be written on human hearts. Instead of gathering harvest grain, the disciples began gathering a spiritual harvest of people from every nation.

### A Message for the Whole World

The miracle of Pentecost revealed that the Gospel was never meant for just one people group. In this single moment:

Language barriers were shattered.

Cultural divisions were bridged.

A global mission was launched.

God's Spirit fell on ordinary believers to accomplish an extraordinary mission, and the Church was born.

## Peter's Bold Declaration

Peter, who only weeks earlier had denied Jesus in fear, now stood with courage before the massive crowd. Filled with the Spirit, he preached about Jesus' life, death, and resurrection with clarity and authority. His words pierced hearts, and the people asked, "What shall we do?"

Peter replied, "**Repent and be baptized, every one of you, in the name of Jesus Christ for the forgiveness of your sins. And you will receive the gift of the Holy Spirit.**" (Acts 2:38, NIV)

That day, about three thousand people believed and were baptized. (Acts 2:41, NIV) The Church was not born in silence, but in fire and transformation.

The first believers quickly became a community of radical love and generosity. They devoted themselves to teaching, prayer, breaking bread together, and caring for those in need. Unity and joy marked their lives, and their witness began to spread like wildfire.

## Pentecost Today

This event is why many churches still celebrate Pentecost Sunday each year. It is not just a remembrance of what God did long ago, but a reminder that the Spirit continues to breathe life into His people. Just as the disciples were empowered to carry the Gospel into the world, so too are we called to live boldly, generously, and faithfully today. Pentecost connects us to that first outpouring, reminding us that the same Spirit who launched the Church then is the Spirit who empowers it now.

## The Holy Spirit: Still Moving Today

The Spirit who filled that upper room is the same Spirit who works in us today. His presence is not confined to history. He comforts, convicts, empowers, and leads.

*Have you ever felt unexplainable peace in the midst of chaos? That's the Spirit reminding you that God is near.*

*Have you ever found the courage to forgive or speak truth when you thought you couldn't? That's the Spirit strengthening you.*

*Have you ever sensed a nudge to reach out to someone at just the right moment? That's the Spirit guiding you.*

The same Spirit who launched the Church at Pentecost continues to shape us, guide us, and send us into the world with boldness.

---

### Community Reflection

- Why do you think God chose Pentecost, with so many nations gathered, to pour out His Spirit?

- In what ways do we sometimes limit the Spirit's work in our churches or daily lives?

- How can we live more like the early Church, marked by boldness, generosity, and unity?

---

## Prayer Prompt: Embracing the Spirit

Reflect on a time when you sensed the Spirit's presence—through peace, courage, conviction, or guidance.

Thank Him for His work in your life. Ask for fresh boldness, more profound wisdom, and an open heart to follow wherever He leads.

## Final Reflections: Living in the Power of the Spirit

Pentecost was not just an ancient event—it was the beginning of God's Spirit dwelling within His people. The same Spirit who gave Peter courage, who united nations in one voice, and who birthed the Church is still moving today.

**As we reflect on Pentecost, may we:**

Remember that God's mission is for every nation and every person.

Live generously, modeling the joy and unity of the early believers.

Stay sensitive to the Spirit's leading, both in extraordinary moments and in daily life.

The Church was never meant to be powered by human effort. From that rushing wind in the upper room to the quiet nudges of the Spirit in our lives today, it is God's Spirit who equips, emboldens, and sends us to carry the message of Jesus to the world.

\*\*\*

## 7.2 Paul's Conversion: Transformation Through Encounter

Scripture Reference: Acts 9:1–31

Saul of Tarsus was a man who thought he knew exactly who he was and what he was meant to do. A zealous Pharisee, he was devoted to upholding the Jewish law with unmatched passion. His reputation spread quickly. The early Christians feared Saul, for he made it his mission to hunt them down, arrest them, and destroy the movement of Jesus once and for all (Acts 9:1–2, NIV). Little did he know that a dramatic and unexpected transformation was about to unfold in his life.

In Saul's mind, he was defending God's honor. Yet in reality, he was fighting against the very One he longed to serve.

## A Blinding Encounter

Picture the scene. Saul marches along the dusty road to Damascus, legal documents in hand, determined to capture more followers of Jesus. The noonday sun blazes overhead, but suddenly a light far brighter than the sun engulfs him. He falls to the ground, shielding his eyes, overwhelmed by terror. Then he hears the voice:

**"Saul, Saul, why do you persecute me?"** (Acts 9:4, NIV)

Shaken and trembling, Saul asks, **"Who are you, Lord?"**

The reply shatters everything he thought he knew:

**"I am Jesus, whom you are persecuting."** (Acts 9:5, NIV)

In that instant, Saul realized that the followers of Jesus he despised were not enemies of God at all. They were His people. The risen Christ Himself had confronted him. When the light faded, Saul opened his eyes—but he could see nothing. Blind, helpless, and utterly dependent, he was led by the very men who had once looked to him for leadership (Acts 9:8, NIV).

## Ananias: A Reluctant Obedience

While Saul sat in darkness for three days, refusing food and drink (Acts 9:9, NIV), God spoke to a disciple named Ananias. The Lord gave him a startling assignment:

**"Go to the house of Judas on Straight Street and ask for a man from Tarsus named Saul, for he is praying."** (Acts 9:11, NIV)

Ananias could hardly believe what he heard. **"Lord, I have heard many reports about this man and all the harm he has done to your holy people in Jerusalem"** (Acts 9:13, NIV). Fear welled up—after all, Saul's reputation was one of violence and persecution. Yet, Ananias's courage was unwavering, a beacon of hope in the midst of fear.

But God assured him:

**"This man is my chosen instrument to proclaim my name to the Gentiles and their kings and to the people of Israel."** (Acts 9:15, NIV)

Ananias obeyed. Stepping into that house, he placed his trembling hands on Saul and called him something Saul had likely never heard from a Christian before:

**"Brother Saul, the Lord Jesus, who appeared to you on the road... has sent me so that you may see again and be filled with the Holy Spirit."** (Acts 9:17, NIV)

Immediately, something like scales fell from Saul's eyes, and he could see again. He rose, was baptized, and began his new life (Acts 9:18, NIV).

Ananias's courage is as much a part of this story as Saul's encounter. Without his obedience, Saul might have remained in darkness. God used one believer's willingness to bridge fear and offer grace to set the stage for the most dramatic transformation in Christian history.

## Paul's Mission: Spreading the Gospel

From that day on, Saul—better known as Paul—became one of the most influential voices in the history of Christianity. His life's mission was turned upside down. Instead of destroying the Church, he devoted himself to planting and nurturing it.

Paul's journeys took him across the Roman Empire, establishing churches in cities like Philippi, Corinth, Thessalonica, and Ephesus. His letters to these communities, written from prisons, ports, and homes, became much of the New Testament, shaping Christian belief and practice for centuries.

But his mission was costly. He was flogged, beaten, imprisoned, and even shipwrecked (2 Corinthians 11:23–27, NIV). Yet Paul never turned back. His conviction remained firm:

**"For to me, to live is Christ and to die is gain."** (Philippians 1:21, NIV)

The man once known for issuing death threats (Acts 9:1, NIV) now breathed life into communities across the world through the message of Jesus Christ.

## What Paul's Story Means for Us

Paul's conversion is more than a dramatic story. It is a reminder of the power of God's grace to transform anyone. His life teaches us that no one is beyond the reach of God's mercy, that God often calls us in directions we never imagined, and that transformation may require surrender but always leads to purpose.

But the story also reminds us of Ananias's role. Transformation rarely happens in isolation. God often uses ordinary people—friends, mentors, fellow believers—to step into the lives of others with encouragement, prayer, and courage. This underscores the vital role each of us plays in the transformative journey of others, making us feel valued and integral.

We may not always be the Saul in the story. Sometimes, we are called to be the Ananias—the one who steps forward in obedience to help another discover God's light.

---

### Community Reflection

- Why do you think God chose Saul, a fierce persecutor, to become one of the greatest apostles?

- How does Ananias's courage remind us of the importance of community in someone's transformation?

- What does Paul's transformation teach us about the power of God's grace to rewrite any story, no matter how broken?

---

## Prayer Prompt: Embracing Change and Calling

Is there an area in your life that needs to shift? Are you resisting a calling because of fear or doubt? Pray for courage to surrender as Paul did, and for faith to embrace the life God is calling you into. Also, ask God to make you attentive like Ananias. To see where He may be asking you to step into someone else's journey with faith and encouragement. Finally, pray for the strength to be an Ananias for others, supporting them in their own transformations.

## Final Reflections: The Acts of the Spirit

From Pentecost's fire to Paul's dramatic conversion, the book of Acts shows us that God delights in transforming lives through the power of His Spirit. It is a story of ordinary people made extraordinary through a divine encounter. It is a story of community, boldness, and mission.

As we continue our own journey of faith, may we welcome the Spirit's guidance, embrace transformation, and live boldly—trusting that the same God who turned Saul into Paul is still writing stories of grace and power through us today.

***

## 7.3 The Council of Jerusalem: Unity in Diversity

Scripture Reference: Acts 15:1–31

Imagine the early Church standing at a turning point. The gospel was spreading quickly beyond Jerusalem. Jews and Gentiles alike were embracing the message of Jesus, but with growth came tension. How could people from such different backgrounds worship together as one?

The pressing question was this: Should Gentile converts be required to obey the full Mosaic Law, including circumcision, to belong to the people of God? (Acts 15:1, NIV)

For many Jewish believers, following Jesus felt like a continuation of their covenant history. The Law had shaped their identity for centuries. To abandon it seemed unthinkable. Yet Paul and Barnabas had seen Gentiles receive the Holy Spirit without following those specific laws (Acts 15:7–9, NIV). God Himself was showing that salvation came through grace, not the strict adherence to the Mosaic Law.

## A Tense but Transformative Debate

The apostles and elders gathered in Jerusalem to resolve this conflict. The room was charged with intensity as both sides made their case. For some, requiring Gentiles to obey the Law seemed necessary to preserve faithfulness. For others, it threatened to place barriers where God had opened doors. This debate, though tense, was transformative. It led to a profound understanding of the gospel and the inclusion of all nations in the Church.

Peter stood up and spoke with boldness:

**"Why do you try to test God by putting on the necks of Gentiles a yoke that neither we nor our ancestors have been able to bear? No, we believe it is through the grace of our Lord Jesus that we are saved, just as they are."** (Acts 15:10–11, NIV)

His words reframed the debate. The Law had never been the source of salvation. God's grace had always been. Paul and Barnabas added their testimony, describing the miracles God had done among the Gentiles (Acts 15:12, NIV). Finally, James, the leader of the Jerusalem church, spoke. Quoting the prophets, he confirmed that God's plan always included the nations (Acts 15:15–18, NIV).

The decision was clear. Gentile believers would not be required to take on the whole Mosaic Law. Instead, they were asked to follow a few practices: abstaining from food sacrificed to idols, from blood, from the meat of strangled animals, and from sexual immorality (Acts 15:19–20, NIV). These guidelines were not conditions for salvation but safeguards for fellowship, helping Jewish and Gentile believers live together in unity by respecting each other's cultural and religious practices.

## Breaking Barriers, Building Bridges

This decision was revolutionary. It declared that the gospel was not bound by ethnicity or culture. The Church was not a Jewish movement alone, but a community where all nations were welcome.

Unity did not mean uniformity. The Council of Jerusalem showed that diversity was not a threat but a testimony. When people of different backgrounds came together in Christ, it revealed the wide embrace of God's Kingdom.

The result was joy. When the letter was delivered to the Gentile believers in Antioch, **"they read it and were glad for its encouraging message"** (Acts 15:31, NIV). What could have fractured the Church instead strengthened it, paving the way for Christianity to spread across cultures and continents.

## Lessons for Today: Embracing Unity in Diversity

The Council of Jerusalem still speaks to us. It reminds us that the heart of the gospel is grace, not added burdens. It calls us to build communities where cultural differences are honored as part of God's design, not seen as obstacles.

When disagreements arise in our churches—whether about tradition, culture, or practice—we can return to this moment as a guide. The early Church chose inclusion over exclusion, grace over gatekeeping, and unity over division.

---

### Community Reflection

- What challenges in today's Church mirror the tensions faced at the Council of Jerusalem?

- How can cultural differences strengthen rather than divide our communities?

- In what ways can we practice grace when disagreements arise?

---

## Prayer Prompt: Seeking Unity in Community

Ask God to help you embrace differences with humility and love. Pray for wisdom when navigating conflict and for a spirit of unity that reflects the heart of the gospel.

## Final Reflections: One Body, Many Members

The Council of Jerusalem shows us that the gospel is for all people. Cultural customs, human traditions, or national identity do not bind it. Salvation is a gift of grace, freely given to Jew and Gentile, rich and poor, insider and outsider alike.

Unity in Christ does not erase diversity—it redeems it. The Church is not strongest when everyone looks and acts the same, but when every culture and background finds belonging in Christ.

**As we reflect on this defining moment, may we:**

Welcome others into fellowship with humility and love.

Resist the temptation to place burdens God has not required.

Celebrate unity that embraces diversity, rooted in the grace of Jesus Christ.

Because the Church is at its best when it reflects the vast, beautiful, and inclusive heart of God.

***

## 7.4 The Fruit of the Spirit: Cultivating Christian Character

Scripture Reference: Galatians 5:13–26

In his letter to the Galatians, Paul paints a vivid contrast between two ways of life. On one side are the works of the flesh—behaviors born from self-centeredness, pride, and rebellion against God. These include jealousy, anger, selfish ambition, impurity, and divisions (Galatians 5:19–21, NIV). On the other side is a life shaped by the Spirit, marked not by chaos and destruction but by qualities that bring life, healing, and hope.

Paul lists them with simple beauty:

**"Love, joy, peace, patience, kindness, goodness, faithfulness, gentleness, and self-control."** (Galatians 5:22–23, NIV)

These are not just moral goals to strive for. They are the visible evidence of the Holy Spirit's transforming presence within us. When the Spirit takes root in our hearts, these qualities begin to grow, slowly reshaping our character and our relationships.

## A Life Shaped by the Spirit

Imagine the Holy Spirit as a gardener. A good gardener does not expect fruit overnight. Instead, he tills the soil, waters faithfully, prunes carefully, and waits patiently for growth. In the same way, spiritual growth takes time. The fruit of the Spirit is cultivated through daily surrender and constant renewal.

Each fruit comes alive in practical ways:

Love reveals itself when we choose compassion, even when it costs us something.

Patience shines when we remain calm in frustration or delay.

Joy grows when we find gratitude in God's goodness rather than in changing circumstances.

Faithfulness shows itself in keeping promises, even when it's inconvenient.

Goodness is lived out in integrity, choosing what is right even when no one else sees.

The Spirit's work is not abstract. It becomes visible in our choices, our relationships, and even the words we speak when life presses us hardest. This transformation, this visible change, is a beacon of hope and a testament to the power of the Spirit in our lives.

## A Community Marked by the Spirit

Paul did not write Galatians to isolated individuals but to a community of believers. The Fruit of the Spirit is not meant only for personal growth. It is intended to shape whole churches. We are all part of this community, and our actions and attitudes contribute to the cultivation of these fruits.

When the Spirit is active in a community, people feel safe, valued, and seen. Kindness becomes the norm rather than the exception. Gentleness and self-control create an environment where trust can flourish. Joy and peace replace rivalry and division. Such communities shine as living testimonies of Christ's love, a beacon of hope in a fractured world.

Imagine a church where love outweighs judgment, where mercy silences gossip, and where joy triumphs over despair. That is the picture Paul paints for the body of Christ.

## Growing in the Fruit of the Spirit

Every garden requires intentional care, and so does our spiritual life. Prayer and Scripture deepen our roots. Acts of service strengthen kindness and goodness. Forgiveness nurtures love and patience. Worship waters our joy. Prayer, in particular, is a powerful tool that can guide us in nurturing the Spirit's fruit in our lives.

Take a moment to reflect: Which of these fruits comes more naturally to you? Which ones feel harder to practice? How can you open yourself to the Spirit's work in those areas?

Paul reminds us that the life of the Spirit is not about striving in our own effort but about surrendering: **"Since we live by the Spirit, let us keep in step with the Spirit."** (Galatians 5:25, NIV)

---

**Community Reflection**

- How does our church or small group reflect the Fruit of the Spirit to those outside our walls?

- Which fruits do we display strongly, and which ones might need more cultivation together?

- What practices—prayer, service, or hospitality—can we embrace as a community to nurture the Spirit's fruit in one another?

---

## Prayer Prompt: Inviting the Spirit's Transformation

Ask God to cultivate the Fruit of the Spirit in your life. Bring to Him the areas where you struggle, and pray for patience as He works in you. Invite Him to make your character a reflection of His love. Pray also for your community, that it may be marked by joy, peace, kindness, and faithfulness, becoming a witness to the world of God's transforming power.

## Final Reflections: A Church That Reflects Christ

From the Council of Jerusalem's pursuit of unity, a significant event in the early Church where leaders gathered to discuss the inclusion of Gentiles in the faith, to Paul's call for Spirit-filled living, a central theme in his letters to various churches, the early Church reminds us that the gospel is not only about correct belief—it is about transformed lives.

The Fruit of the Spirit demonstrates to the world what it means to belong to Christ:

The gospel transcends culture and unites people from every background.

Love, joy, and peace are not optional extras—they are markers of life in the Spirit.

True transformation comes not through striving but through surrender to God's work within us.

As we move forward in faith, may we embrace differences with grace, pursue growth with intention, and let both our lives and our communities reflect the beauty of the Spirit's fruit. For when we do, we become living testimonies of God's love—**"like a tree planted by streams of water, which yields its fruit in season and whose leaf does not wither"** (Psalm 1:3, NIV).

***

## 7.5 The Armor of God: Spiritual Readiness and Protection

Scripture Reference: Ephesians 6:10–18

Life's greatest battles often arrive without warning. They can be personal crises that shake us to the core, such as the loss of a loved one or a sudden health scare. More often, they creep in quietly—waves of discouragement, nagging doubts, or subtle temptations. In those moments, we may feel unprepared, our faith shaken, and our focus blurred.

But Paul gives us a powerful image to anchor our strength:

**"Put on the full armor of God, so that you can take your stand against the devil's schemes."** (Ephesians 6:11, NIV)

This is not armor of steel or leather. It is spiritual protection. God's truth and promises wrapped around us, equipping believers to face struggles both seen and unseen.

Paul describes each piece:

The **belt of truth** grounds us in honesty and integrity, holding everything else together like the belt of a soldier fastening his armor.

The **breastplate of righteousness** guards our hearts from corruption and compromise, protecting what is most vital.

The **shield of faith** blocks the flaming arrows of fear, lies, and doubt that seek to pierce our confidence in God.

The **helmet of salvation** secures our minds with assurance, reminding us daily that our hope and identity are safe in Christ.

The **sword of the Spirit**—the Word of God—is both defense and offense. It is a defensive weapon when we use it to counter the enemy's attacks and temptations. It is an offensive weapon when we use it to share the gospel and bring others to Christ. This piece of the armor equips us not just to endure, but to advance with wisdom and power.

Paul's description is more than poetic imagery. It is a practical call to live prepared, clothed daily in the strength that God provides, empowering us to face life's challenges with confidence and capability.

## Standing Firm in Life's Battles

Paul reminds us that readiness is not passive. Just as soldiers train with discipline before stepping onto the battlefield, Christians must cultivate habits that keep us spiritually strong.

Prayer roots us in God's presence, keeping us aware of His guidance.

Scripture sharpens our minds, helping us recognize truth and resist deception.

Community surrounds us with encouragement and accountability, reminding us we are never alone.

The enemy rarely attacks through obvious threats. More often, the danger comes in distraction, division, or small compromises that weaken our focus. To put on the armor of God is to stay awake, alert, and anchored in faith, ready to stand firm no matter what comes.

## A Community Strengthened Together

It is important to remember that Paul wrote these words to a church, not just to individuals. Spiritual battles are best faced side by side, as the people of God, fostering a sense of support and connection.

The prayers of others sustain us when our own words falter.

Encouragement from friends strengthens us when our faith feels thin.

The witness of the whole Church proclaims that no believer stands alone.

When the body of Christ stands together—each one clothed in armor—we become an unshakable force, not because of our strength, but because of the God who equips and defends us.

---

## Community Reflection

- Which part of the armor of God do you find most difficult to "put on" consistently, and why?

- How can we, as a church or small group, support one another in staying spiritually strong and alert?

- What everyday practices can help us recognize and resist subtle distractions or compromises that weaken faith?

---

## Strengthening Your Spiritual Readiness

Reflect for a moment:

*Which piece of the armor do you most need in this season of life?*

*Are you daily training your faith through prayer, Scripture, and fellowship?*

*Who in your community helps strengthen your walk with Christ?*

## Prayer Prompt: Embracing Spiritual Readiness

Ask God to equip you with His armor each day. Pray for clarity to recognize the enemy's subtle schemes, strength to resist temptation, and courage to encourage others in their battles.

## Final Reflections: Living Fully Armed in Christ

The armor of God is more than a metaphor. It is a way of living. Each piece represents a truth that steadies us: His Word, His righteousness, His salvation, His Spirit. Together, they give us the confidence not just to survive life's trials but to stand with courage and resilience.

**As we reflect on Paul's words, may we:**

Put on truth in a world of deception.

Guard our hearts with righteousness.

Raise faith as a shield against fear.

Stand boldly, knowing God fights for us.

The armor of God is not a burden. It is freedom. And when we wear it faithfully, we discover the strength to stand firm, no matter the battle.

***

## 7.6 Revelation's Promise: Hope in the Midst of Persecution

Scripture Reference: Revelation 7:16–17; Revelation 21:1–5

The book of Revelation, with its vivid symbols and apocalyptic imagery, can feel mysterious—even overwhelming. Yet at its heart, it is not a book of fear, but of hope.

Picture John, the beloved disciple, banished to the rocky island of Patmos. He was exiled for his testimony about Jesus, cut off from the churches he loved, living in isolation under Roman persecution (Revelation 1:9, NIV). To a man surrounded by hardship and despair, God gave a vision that lifted his eyes beyond suffering to see heaven's throne, the victorious Lamb, and a renewed creation where all things would be made new.

This vision was not only about the distant future; it was a call to perseverance, courage, and faithfulness in the present.

## Victory Through the Lamb

At the heart of Revelation's vision stands the Lamb—Jesus Christ—who was slain yet reigns victorious. It is a paradox: power revealed through sacrifice, victory achieved through suffering. This unique victory is a testament to the divine nature of Christ and the depth of God's love for us.

**"For the Lamb at the center of the throne will be their shepherd; 'he will lead them to springs of living water.' And God will wipe away every tear from their eyes."** (Revelation 7:17, NIV)

For the early Christians, many of whom faced imprisonment, loss of livelihood, or even death, these words were life itself. Their suffering was not meaningless. Their faith was not in vain. The Lamb had already won.

## Finding Strength in the Promise of Victory

Every generation of believers has faced trials that test faith—whether persecution, cultural pressure, grief, or doubt. The early Christians receiving John's letter were pressed on every side. Yet, Revelation reminded them of this unshakable truth: **Christ has already won.**

The same assurance steadies us today. When life feels uncertain, when the weight of fear or struggle threatens to overwhelm, we remember that the end of the story is already written. The Lamb is victorious. God will wipe every tear. The night will not last forever.

**So we ask ourselves:**

*How do we hold onto hope when the world feels uncertain?*

*What promises of God anchor us when life feels overwhelming?*

*How can we live today with the confidence that ultimate victory belongs to Christ?*

## Symbols of Hope and Renewal

Revelation uses images to communicate truths deeper than words alone:

**The dragon and the beast** represent forces of evil and oppression—reminders that behind earthly struggles lies a greater spiritual battle.

**The New Jerusalem** is a radiant city descending from heaven, where God dwells with His people (Revelation 21:1-3, NIV). Its streets gleam with gold, its gates are made of pearl, and its foundations sparkle with precious stones (Revelation 21:18-21, NIV). But the beauty of this city is not in its materials—it is in its presence. There is no temple, because God Himself dwells among His people. There is no sun or moon, for the glory of God gives it light (Revelation 21:22-23, NIV). In this city, there is no more mourning, crying, or pain. Brokenness is healed, and death is no more (Revelation 21:4, NIV). It is a vision of home, where every longing heart finally finds rest.

**The river of life and tree of life** flow through the city, bringing healing to the nations (Revelation 22:1-2, NIV). What humanity lost in Eden is restored—perfect communion with God, unbroken peace with one another, and creation renewed in harmony.

These images are not meant to frighten but to inspire endurance. They declare that evil will not have the last word and that God's presence will one day fill the earth.

## Community Reflection

- How can we encourage one another with the hope of Christ's victory when life feels overwhelming?

- In what ways can our communities reflect the "New Jerusalem" by becoming places of healing, restoration, and light?

- What practices help us keep our eyes on God's promises instead of our present struggles?

## Prayer Prompt: Holding Onto Hope

Bring before God your fears, uncertainties, and struggles. Ask Him to anchor you in the promise of His victory. Pray for strength to persevere with faith, courage, and peace, trusting that He will make all things new.

## Final Reflections: Living in Readiness and Hope

From Paul's call to put on the Armor of God to John's vision of Christ's triumph, Scripture reminds us of this truth:

We are called to live prepared in faith.

We are part of a story much bigger than ourselves, a story of faith, perseverance, and victory. Each of us has a unique role to play in this grand narrative.

We can endure because God's promises never fail. They are not fleeting or conditional, but enduring and unwavering. As we face trials and tribulations, we can take comfort in the fact that God's promises are steadfast and will always come to pass.

As we walk forward, may we:

Stand firm in faith, clothed in God's armor.

Find comfort in the assurance that Christ has already won.

Live as people of hope, reflecting God's light even in difficult times.

Because no matter how long the night may seem, dawn is coming. And when it comes, it will never end.

# Chapter 8

# Wisdom and Poetic Books

There are seasons in life when we don't need another law, a dramatic miracle, or a prophetic warning—we need wisdom. The Wisdom and Poetic Books of the Bible, with their timeless relevance, speak to those everyday moments of decision, doubt, and desire. They are prayers when words fail, songs for both joy and sorrow, and proverbs that turn ordinary choices into lasting lessons.

These writings remind us that faith is not only about grand events but also about how we live, speak, and think in the quiet rhythms of daily life. In Proverbs, Psalms, Job, Ecclesiastes, and the Song of Songs, we encounter

God's wisdom not only for kings and prophets but for every heart seeking guidance, comfort, and meaning, reassuring us that God's wisdom guides us in every aspect of our lives.

\*\*\*

## 8.1 Proverbs: The Path to Wisdom

Scripture Reference: Proverbs 1:1–7; Proverbs 9:10; Proverbs 18:21

I remember stumbling across an old copy of Proverbs at a garage sale as a teenager. Its frayed cover and yellowed pages hinted at years of use, but something about it drew me in. As I flipped through its short, piercing sayings, I was surprised by their power. Even then, I sensed these words were not just relics of an ancient time, but principles for living that felt as relevant as the choices I faced each day.

The book of Proverbs is like a treasure chest of wisdom, each verse a jewel offering guidance for a life well lived. It contrasts wisdom and folly, discipline and recklessness, showing that every choice we make shapes our path.

### The Power of Proverbs in Daily Life

In ancient Israel, Proverbs was foundational. Often attributed to King Solomon, these sayings were used by parents, elders, and scribes to train the next generation. They shaped families, guided communities, and even influenced kings, embedding moral and ethical principles into everyday life.

Proverbs begins by declaring its purpose:

**"The proverbs of Solomon, son of David, king of Israel: for gaining wisdom and instruction; for understanding words of insight; for receiving instruction in prudent behavior, doing what is right and just and fair."** (Proverbs 1:1–3, NIV)

At the heart of Proverbs is discipline—the ability to govern our actions, thoughts, and desires. It elevates integrity, calling us to live honestly and align our choices with what is right. Most importantly, it introduces a foundational truth:

**"The fear of the Lord is the beginning of wisdom, and knowledge of the Holy One is understanding."** (Proverbs 9:10, NIV)

This "fear" is not terror, but reverence—an awe-filled respect for God's authority that places Him at the center of all accurate understanding.

The book also emphasizes the immense power of words. Speech is never neutral; it can build up or destroy, heal or wound:

**"The tongue has the power of life and death, and those who love it will eat its fruit."** (Proverbs 18:21, NIV)

And again:

**"Gracious words are a honeycomb, sweet to the soul and healing to the bones."** (Proverbs 16:24, NIV)

These truths highlight how wisdom is woven into the very fabric of everyday life.

## Applying Proverbs to Modern Life

Proverbs is not just a collection of ancient sayings; it's a practical guide for our daily decisions. Its wisdom is not confined to the past; it's alive and applicable to our lives today.

It teaches us to think long-term rather than react in the moment, to choose wisdom over impulse, and to trust in God's leading instead of relying solely on ourselves:

**"Trust in the Lord with all your heart and lean not on your own understanding; in all your ways submit to Him, and He will make your paths straight."** (Proverbs 3:5-6, NIV)

In relationships, Proverbs calls us to patience, kindness, humility, and the value of listening:

**"To answer before listening—that is folly and shame."** (Proverbs 18:13, NIV)

In daily habits, it emphasizes discipline and consistency:

**"Go to the ant, you sluggard; consider its ways and be wise!"** (Proverbs 6:6, NIV)

**"The plans of the diligent lead to profit as surely as haste leads to poverty."** (Proverbs 21:5, NIV)

These timeless lessons remind us that small, consistent choices shape who we become.

When embraced, Proverbs transcends being an ancient collection of sayings. It becomes a transformative roadmap for building character, nurturing faith, and living a life of purpose and intentionality, empowering us to live with intention and inspiration.

## Prayer Prompt: Proverbial Wisdom in Action

Choose a proverb that resonates with you today. As you reflect, ask God:

*How does this truth apply to my life right now?*

*What changes can I make to align more closely with this wisdom?*

Pray for understanding and clarity, trusting that as you walk in wisdom, you are aligning yourself with God's design for a meaningful life.

---

### Community Reflection

- Which proverb has most shaped your life, and why?

- Why do you think Proverbs calls "the fear of the Lord" the beginning of wisdom?

- How do words—spoken or written—shape our relationships and communities today?

---

## Final Reflections: Choosing Wisdom Daily

Proverbs reminds us that wisdom is not about acquiring knowledge for its own sake. It is about shaping our character and guiding our daily decisions.

**"The wise in heart accept commands, but a chattering fool comes to ruin."** (Proverbs 10:8, NIV)

It teaches us to live with reverence before God, integrity before others, and discipline within ourselves.

Wisdom, as Proverbs shows us, is not a one-time choice but a daily pursuit. Each decision, whether in our words, habits, or relationships, moves us toward wisdom or away from it.

May we treasure the wisdom God has given, guard our speech carefully, and walk in reverence before Him, trusting that every step in wisdom leads us closer to peace, purpose, and blessing.

\*\*\*

## 8.2 Ecclesiastes: Seeking Meaning in a Transient World

Scripture Reference: Ecclesiastes 1:2; Ecclesiastes 2:11; Ecclesiastes 3:11–13; Ecclesiastes 12:13

The first time I read Ecclesiastes, I felt a strange mix of bewilderment and intrigue. Its opening words startled me:

**"Vanity of vanities! All is vanity!"** (Ecclesiastes 1:2, NIV)

It immediately made me pause. What was Solomon, the wisest man who ever lived, trying to tell us?

Ecclesiastes confronts the stark reality that much of what we pursue—wealth, success, pleasure—ultimately leaves us unfulfilled. It strips away illusions of control, forcing us to reevaluate what truly matters.

### Life's Fleeting Nature

The author, traditionally believed to be King Solomon, explores the cycles of time, work, and human ambition. He observes how life feels repetitive and fragile:

**"What has been will be again, what has been done will be done again; there is nothing new under the sun."** (Ecclesiastes 1:9, NIV)

Generations come and go, the sun rises and sets, and human striving continues without lasting satisfaction. He reflects that even wealth and accomplishments, though impressive, cannot guarantee joy:

**"Yet when I surveyed all that my hands had done and what I had toiled to achieve, everything was meaningless, a chasing after the wind."** (Ecclesiastes 2:11, NIV)

Even pleasure, though enjoyable, leaves the heart unsatisfied. Ecclesiastes does not shy away from this sobering truth. It reminds us that life "under the sun" is fleeting.

## Finding Purpose Beyond Vanity

Yet Ecclesiastes is not without hope. Beneath the laments lies a call to shift our focus toward what endures. Solomon concludes with clarity:

**"Fear God and keep His commandments, for this is the duty of all mankind."** (Ecclesiastes 12:13, NIV)

Along the way, he points to simple joys as gifts from God:

**"I know that there is nothing better for people than to be happy and to do good while they live. That each of them may eat and drink, and find satisfaction in all their toil—this is the gift of God."** (Ecclesiastes 3:12–13, NIV)

And perhaps most profound, he reminds us that God **"has made everything beautiful in its time. He has also set eternity in the human heart."** (Ecclesiastes 3:11, NIV)

Here lies the paradox: we long for something eternal in a world that is temporary. That longing points us to God.

## Applying Ecclesiastes to Modern Life

Even in our modern, achievement-driven culture, Ecclesiastes speaks directly to us. We often find ourselves chasing wealth, recognition, or comfort, yet still feel restless. This book challenges us to ask: are we building our lives on things that fade, or on the God who remains?

It teaches us to slow down and savor the present: a meal with friends, meaningful work, the beauty of creation. It urges us to accept that some things remain outside our control, and that peace comes not from striving but from trusting God's timing.

## Living with Eternal Perspective

As we navigate careers, relationships, and personal growth, Ecclesiastes invites us to pause and reflect:

*Are we chasing things that do not last?*

*Do we take time to appreciate life's simple gifts?*

*Are we seeking fulfillment in God, or in temporary success?*

## Prayer Prompt: Finding Meaning Beyond Vanity

Ask God to help you see beyond the distractions of this world and to focus on what truly lasts. Pray for contentment in simple blessings, clarity to see His eternal plan, and a heart anchored in Him.

---

### Community Reflection

- Why do you think we so often chase after things we know cannot fully satisfy?

- How can we remind one another to slow down and embrace God's simple gifts in daily life?

- In what ways does the longing for eternity in our hearts (Ecclesiastes 3:11) shape the way we live today?

---

## Final Reflections on Proverbs and Ecclesiastes

Together, Proverbs and Ecclesiastes provide us with a balanced perspective. Proverbs teaches us how to live wisely in our daily decisions, while Ecclesiastes reminds us of life's brevity and directs us toward eternity. This balance guides us in our spiritual journey.

Wisdom equips us to live well, but reverence for God gives life meaning. True fulfillment does not come from what we achieve, but from the God who created us for Himself.

$$***$$

## 8.3 Job's Suffering: Trusting God Amidst Trials

Scripture Reference: Job 1:1–42:17

Imagine a man whose life could not have been more blessed. Job had wealth beyond measure, a thriving family, and a reputation for integrity. He was known for his devotion to God, living a life many admired. Everything seemed secure until, in a single moment, his world shattered.

One day, a divine conversation took place in the heavenly courts. Satan challenged Job's faithfulness, suggesting that his devotion was tied only to his prosperity. With God's permission, Job's life was overturned.

His wealth was stolen, his children tragically lost, and his body covered in painful sores. Once surrounded by abundance, he now sat in ashes, broken and alone (Job 1:13–22, NIV).

Job's first response was not rebellion but worship. In his grief, he declared:

**"The Lord gave and the Lord has taken away; may the name of the Lord be praised."** (Job 1:21, NIV)

But as the suffering stretched on, Job began to wrestle with questions that have echoed through history: Why do the innocent suffer? Where is justice in pain? How can faith survive when everything is lost?

## Friends and Flawed Comfort

Job's friends came, sitting with him in silence for seven days (Job 2:13, NIV). Their presence at first was compassionate, a silent support in his grief. However, their understanding of suffering was limited, and they soon began to accuse him. Surely, they reasoned, he must have sinned to deserve such punishment. Yet Job knew their words were wrong. His protests grew raw and honest. He poured out his lament, questioning God, longing for answers, but never cursing Him (Job 2:9-10, NIV).

## A Response from the Whirlwind

Finally, after chapters of silence, God spoke—not with explanations, but with overwhelming presence.

**"Where were you when I laid the earth's foundation? Tell me, if you understand."** (Job 38:4, NIV)

God's response was not about *why* Job suffered but about *who* God is. He spoke of creation's vastness, mysteries beyond human understanding, and His sovereign wisdom. Job was humbled. He realized his perspective was limited, while God's purposes reached far beyond what he could see.

Job confessed:

**"Surely I spoke of things I did not understand, things too wonderful for me to know."** (Job 42:3, NIV)

His pain was still real, but his posture had changed. Job found peace not in explanations but in the transformative power of God's presence. In the end, the Lord restored Job's fortunes, giving him twice as much as he had before (Job 42:10, NIV).

Yet the truest restoration was not in his wealth. It was in his faith, tested and refined like gold, reassuring us of God's comforting presence in our own trials.

## Wrestling with Suffering in Our Own Lives

Job's story is more than ancient history. It mirrors our own struggles. There are seasons when faith is tested, when life feels unfair, and when God seems silent.

But Job's journey reminds us:

Faith is not about having all the answers—it is about holding onto God in the unknown.

Honest prayers, even when filled with doubt, are still acts of worship.

God's presence is more potent than explanations.

Perhaps you have walked through a season of loss or disappointment, asking questions like Job. His story encourages us, not with the promise of a pain-free life, but with the assurance that God is still present, even in the ashes.

## Prayer Prompt: Trusting in the Unknown

Bring your questions, pain, and doubts before God. Even if His answers are not what you expect, ask Him for the faith to trust His presence. Pray for peace to see beyond the suffering and courage to hold onto Him in the unknown.

---

### Community Reflection

- Why do you think Job refused to curse God, even when he questioned Him?

- How does God's response shift the focus from "why" to "who"?

- Have you ever experienced peace not because the situation changed, but because your perspective did?

Reflect on a time when you found peace in the midst of suffering, not because the situation improved, but because your understanding of it did. Share your reflections with the community to foster a sense of shared experience and empathy.

## Final Reflections on Job

Job's story teaches us that suffering does not mean abandonment. God's silence is not His absence, and His presence is more sustaining than explanations. Job's faith was not destroyed by loss. It was reshaped into something more resilient and profound, inspiring us to face our own trials with courage and trust.

As we face our own trials, may we learn to pray honestly, trust deeply, and rest in the God who is greater than our pain. True hope is not found in avoiding suffering, but in knowing the One who walks with us through it.

*** 

## 8.4 The Psalms: Finding Refuge in God's Presence

*Scripture Reference: Psalms 1–150*

There is something about the Psalms that makes them feel deeply personal. They do not just recount history or offer instruction; they give voice to the deepest emotions of the human soul.

Imagine sitting beside David, a man after God's own heart, as he pours out his life before God; sometimes in soaring praise, sometimes in raw anguish, sometimes in quiet trust. The Psalms capture the full spectrum of what it means to live with faith in a broken world.

Some psalms overflow with gratitude and confidence: **"The Lord is my shepherd, I lack nothing."** (Psalm 23:1, NIV)

Others cry out from the depths of despair: **"My God, my God, why have you forsaken me?"** (Psalm 22:1, NIV)

Still others invite us into reverence and stillness: **"Be still, and know that I am God."** (Psalm 46:10, NIV)

And many burst with joy and thanksgiving: **"Enter his gates with thanksgiving and his courts with praise; give thanks to him and praise his name."** (Psalm 100:4, NIV)

No matter what season of life we find ourselves in, there is a psalm that gives us words when we cannot see our own.

## Psalms in Worship and Reflection

For thousands of years, the Psalms have been at the heart of both public worship and private devotion. They were sung in the temple, recited in homes, and treasured in personal prayer. Their honesty, rhythm, and beauty make them timeless companions for every circumstance, connecting us to a rich tradition of faith and worship.

When life overwhelms us, the Psalms remind us: **"God is our refuge and strength, an ever-present help in trouble."** (Psalm 46:1, NIV)

When our hearts break, they assure us: **"The Lord is close to the brokenhearted and saves those who are crushed in spirit."** (Psalm 34:18, NIV)

When fear grips us, they proclaim: **"The Lord is my light and my salvation—whom shall I fear?"** (Psalm 27:1, NIV)

The Psalms remind us that God is not only the Lord of the nations but also the shepherd of every individual soul.

## Bringing the Psalms into Our Lives

The Psalms are not just meant to be read; they are intended to be lived. They invite us to let their words shape the rhythm of our days. You can begin your morning with a psalm, letting it set the tone for your day. In times of trial, seek out a psalm of lament that echoes your grief. In seasons of joy, turn to psalms of thanksgiving that lift your praise. Use their words as prayers, transforming ancient verses into living conversations with God.

In doing so, the Psalms become more than poetry; they become transformative pathways into God's presence, inspiring us and filling us with hope.

## Prayer Prompt: Psalm Reflection Exercise

Choose one psalm and read it slowly, perhaps even aloud. As you reflect, ask yourself: What does this psalm reveal about who God is? How does it mirror my own emotions or circumstances? How can I carry its message into my daily choices and prayers?

Then turn the psalm into your own prayer thanking God for His presence, asking Him for strength, and trusting Him with both your burdens and joys.

---

### Community Reflection

- Which psalm has spoken most deeply to you in a time of joy or sorrow?

- Why do you think the Psalms continue to feel so relevant across generations?

- How can we use the Psalms to enrich both personal prayer and communal worship today?

---

## Final Reflections on Job and the Psalms

From Job's suffering to the raw honesty of the Psalms, these writings remind us that faith is not about having unshakable certainty—it is about clinging to God in every season. They show us that prayer is not only about praise but also includes lament, doubt, confession, and thanksgiving.

Together, Job and the Psalms testify that God is our refuge, our foundation, and our hope.

As you walk through both struggles and victories, may you learn perseverance from Job, find comfort in the Psalms, and trust that God's presence is with you always—through every valley and on every mountaintop.

***

## 8.5 Song of Solomon: Love and Intimacy in Divine Context

*Scripture Reference: Song of Solomon 1–8*

Love is often described as a mystery, a longing that stirs the soul, a fire that burns deeply yet refines beautifully. Nowhere in Scripture is this passion and devotion more vividly portrayed than in the Song of Solomon. Unlike any other book in the Bible, it celebrates the beauty of love, intimacy, and commitment with poetic imagery that is both tender and bold.

As you read its verses, you enter a world where love is cherished, honored, and fiercely pursued. This is not a love of fleeting emotions or shallow attraction, but one rooted in admiration, joy, and sacred covenant. Its poetry bursts with images of springtime renewal, fragrant gardens, and steadfast devotion—symbols of love that are tender yet unbreakable.

### Love as a Reflection of the Divine

The Song of Solomon beautifully reflects the divine nature of love. It is a testament to the sacred bond between God and His people, a faithful love that is both pursuing and unwavering. The Song of Solomon paints a picture of romantic love that is deeply personal yet profoundly sacred. Desire and devotion are not outside of God's plan; they are part of His design, meant to be experienced within relationships of trust and covenantal commitment.

The words between the lovers overflow with admiration and belonging:

**"I am my beloved's, and my beloved is mine."** (Song of Solomon 6:3, NIV)

But this book has always carried more than one layer of meaning. In Jewish tradition, it has been seen as a celebration of God's covenant love for Israel. In Christian thought, it has often been read as a reflection of Christ's love for His Church. Both interpretations point us to the same truth: God's love is faithful, pursuing, and

unwavering.

## The Symbolism of Love and Commitment

Understanding the cultural and historical backdrop of the Song of Solomon deepens its message. Gardens and vineyards, recurring images in the text, represent fertility, intimacy, and the cultivation of love. The elaborate wedding customs of the time remind us that marriage was not just a social contract but a covenant; an enduring union of loyalty and devotion.

This context highlights an important truth: love is not just about passion; it requires cultivation. Like a well-tended vineyard, love thrives through patience, care, and mutual respect. It is an active commitment that grows stronger with attention and faithfulness. For instance, showing appreciation, spending quality time together, and communicating openly and honestly are all ways to cultivate love in a relationship.

## Love as a Divine Gift

In a culture that often reduces love to fleeting attraction or temporary emotion, the Song of Solomon calls us back to God's vision. It reminds us that true love is not shallow, selfish, or seasonal. It is faithful, sacrificial, and enduring. It is a love that weathers both joy and hardship, providing us with a sense of security and stability.

Whether you are in a relationship, longing for one, or reflecting on love in a different season of life, this book speaks wisdom into what it means to love well. It reminds us that love is one of God's greatest gifts, meant to be honored, celebrated, and cherished as holy.

## Reflecting on Love in Your Own Life

As you consider the Song of Solomon, take a moment to reflect on how your relationships mirror God's covenant love. Are you cultivating love that is marked by respect, faithfulness, and kindness? How does God's faithful love shape the way you give and receive love in your daily life? This introspective reflection will deepen your understanding of love's divine nature.

## Community Reflection

- How can we as a faith community encourage relationships that reflect God's covenant love—faithful, patient, and honoring?

- In what ways can the Church celebrate and support marriages, families, and friendships as reflections of divine love?

- How does seeing the Song of Solomon as an allegory of God's love for His people shape the way we view love in our own community?

## Prayer Prompt: Embracing Love as a Gift

Pray that God would help you cultivate love that honors Him—whether in friendships, family, or romantic relationships. Ask for wisdom to build relationships marked by faithfulness, grace, and commitment. Thank Him for His love, which is the model and foundation for all true love.

## Final Reflections on the Song of Solomon

From Proverbs' wisdom to Ecclesiastes' reflection, from Job's perseverance to the Psalms' honesty, the Song of Solomon adds a unique voice to the wisdom and poetic books of Scripture. It reminds us that love itself is sacred. Romantic devotion, expressed with purity and passion, reflects God's covenant with His people.

As we embrace love in its many forms—familial, romantic, or divine—may we see it as one of God's greatest gifts. May our relationships be marked by joy, faithfulness, and grace. And may we never forget that at the heart of all love worth celebrating is the God who first loved us.

***

## 8.6 Lamentations: Expressing Grief and Finding Hope

*Scripture Reference: Lamentations 1–5*

The book of Lamentations begins with haunting imagery: **"How deserted lies the city, once so full of people!"** (Lamentations 1:1, NIV).

Jerusalem, once alive with worship and celebration, now stood silent and ruined. The year was 586 BCE, the year the Babylonians invaded, destroyed the Temple, and sent many into exile. For the people of Israel, this was more than the collapse of a city. It was the collapse of identity, security, and spiritual foundation. Families were scattered, the streets were filled with mourning, and grief became the language of survival.

The book gives voice to this collective sorrow. It does not mask pain behind easy answers, nor does it minimize the devastation. Instead, it allows lament to rise from the ashes, reminding us that expressing grief is an essential part of faith.

### The Tension Between Grief and Hope

Lamentations is raw and unfiltered; a poetic cry from hearts wrestling with suffering and searching for meaning. The grief is unrelenting: **"My eyes fail from weeping, I am in torment within"** (Lamentations 2:11, NIV). Yet in the middle of these laments comes one of the most profound declarations of hope in all of Scripture:

**"The steadfast love of the Lord never ceases; His mercies never come to an end; they are new every morning; great is Your faithfulness."** (Lamentations 3:22–23, NIV)

This is the paradox of Lamentations. The sorrow is deep and undeniable, but hope is not extinguished. Even in devastation, the poet clings to God's character—His mercy, His love, and His faithfulness.

## The Structure of Lamentations: Finding Order in Chaos

Though filled with anguish, the book is not chaotic in form. Each chapter is written as an acrostic poem, using the Hebrew alphabet as a framework (Lamentations 1–4). This structure reflects a human desire to bring order into the chaos of grief. Even in lament, there is intention, rhythm, and worship.

It teaches us that lament is not simply venting emotion. It is a sacred practice of bringing pain before God in a way that trusts Him to hold it.

## The Power of Lament in Our Own Lives

Many of us struggle to express grief honestly, fearing it shows weakness or lack of faith. Yet Lamentations permits us to weep, to question, and to wrestle openly with God. It takes great courage to express honest lament. It is not faithlessness—it is faith expressed in the midst of brokenness.

Grief and hope are not opposites. In fact, Lamentations shows us that hope often shines brightest through grief. To lament is to trust that our cries are heard and that God's presence remains, even when His purposes are not clear. This hope, even in the midst of grief, can be a source of great encouragement.

## Finding Strength in Honest Lament

Each of us carries places of grief, loss, disappointment, seasons of silence, or hardship. Lamentations invites us to speak these aloud to God, not suppress them. In naming sorrow, we make space for healing. And in remembering God's mercies, we anchor our hope beyond what we see in the moment. This is where the support of our faith community becomes crucial, providing a sense of connection and support.

## Community Reflection

- How can communities of faith create safe spaces for people to express grief and lament without judgment?

- What does it look like to practice lament together—in worship, in small groups, or in times of collective hardship?

- How does remembering God's steadfast love and mercy (Lamentations 3:22-23, NIV) help us walk with others through seasons of loss and sorrow?

## Prayer Prompt: Finding Hope in Grief

Bring your struggles, sorrows, and doubts before God in prayer. Ask Him to meet you in your pain, to remind you of His nearness, and to give you courage to grieve honestly. Pray that His mercies would renew your strength each morning and that His faithfulness would carry you through seasons of darkness.

Consider praying for specific situations in your life where you need to practice lament and trust in God's faithfulness. For example, if you're going through a season of loss, pray for the strength to express your grief honestly and the faith to believe in God's steadfast love and mercy.

## Final Reflections on Love and Lament

From the celebration of love in the Song of Solomon to the sorrow-filled cries of Lamentations, these books reveal the full breadth of human experience before God. Love is God's gift, meant to be honored, cherished, and cultivated. Grief is also part of life, but even in the darkest hours, hope is never extinguished.

Together, these books remind us that God is present in both the joy of love and the sorrow of lament. As we reflect, may we:

Seek relationships that reflect God's faithful love.

Allow ourselves to bring grief before Him with honesty.

Hold tightly to hope, remembering that His mercies are new every morning (Lamentations 3:22–23, NIV).

**Because in both love and lament, He is near.**

# Conclusion

As we reach the final pages of this journey through the timeless stories of the Bible, I want to pause—not simply to end, but to **reflect**. I hope that, as you've read, you've discovered new insights, experienced moments of clarity, and felt God's presence speaking into your life in a personal and meaningful way.

When I first set out to write this book, I wasn't just thinking about history or theology. I was thinking about you, the reader longing for meaning, direction, and reassurance that faith is not only something we read about but something we live. These stories are not relics of an ancient world. They are a living testament to our human experience: **our struggles, our questions, our moments of despair, and our moments of hope.**

As I wrote, I found myself reflecting on my own journey. Times when I wrestled with doubt, when I needed direction, when I felt God's nearness, and when I wondered if He was silent. Perhaps you've felt the same. Maybe you saw yourself in Abraham's faith, Job's perseverance, or the prodigal's return. Maybe you were challenged by Jesus' radical call to love, forgive, and live with humility.

Through every story, one truth has shone brightly: **God is always at work**. Even in chaos, betrayal, exile, or suffering, His redemptive love breaks through. The people of Scripture remind us that God's story never stops with failure. It always bends toward restoration.

And that is what I want to leave you with—**HOPE**.

Because no matter where you are right now—strong in faith or struggling to hold on—God's story isn't finished with you yet. The same God who parted the Red Sea, who sat with Job in his pain, who welcomed the prodigal home, and who empowered the disciples at Pentecost is the same God who walks with you today.

So, as you move forward:

**When you face trials, remember Joseph**—who endured betrayal yet held onto God's dream.

**When forgiveness feels impossible, remember the father** who ran to embrace his lost son.

**When you feel uncertain, remember the disciples**—afraid and doubting, yet met by the risen Christ.

**And when hope feels far away, remember Revelation's promise:** the Lamb has already overcome.

Most importantly, remember this—**you are not alone.**

God never meant for us to walk in Faith in isolation. These stories live on because they remind us that we belong to something greater—a legacy of faith stretching across centuries and a community that still wrestles, questions, prays, and believes together.

**You are not alone in this journey.**

As we close this book, my prayer is that this is not really an ending but a beginning:

May the lessons you've learned take root in your heart.

May they inspire you to live with **courage, extend grace, and trust God** even in the unknown.

May they remind you that **His love is constant, His wisdom steady, and His presence unshakable.**

Thank you for taking this journey with me. Thank you for opening your heart to be challenged, encouraged, and renewed. And as you step into tomorrow, remember that you play a vital role in continuing God's story.

May you walk boldly in the truth that **God's story is still being written in your life.**

**And may you always know—His presence goes before you, His promises surround you, and His love will never fail. You are never alone, for He is always with you.**

# Closing Prayer

Lord, thank You for the stories that remind us of who You are and who we are called to be. As we leave these pages, may Your Word remain alive in our hearts. Give us courage in trials, joy in Your presence, and hope that never fades. May our lives reflect Your love to the world around us.

In Jesus' name, Amen.

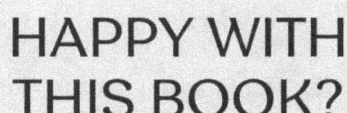

# HAPPY WITH THIS BOOK?

—— Let Me Know ——

If this book has blessed you, would you take a moment to leave a review and help others discover its encouragement?

<<   Scan here to leave a quick review   >>

GOD BLESS YOU

# References

- Zondervan Academic. *Understanding the Creation Story from Genesis.* Retrieved from https://zondervanacademic.com/blog/understanding-the-creation-story-from-genesis

- Wikipedia. *Fall of Man.* Retrieved from https://en.wikipedia.org/wiki/Fall_of_man

- Biblical Life Lessons. *The Significance of Noah's Ark in Christian Symbolism.* Retrieved from https://biblicallifelessons.com/the-significance-of-noahs-ark-in-christian-symbolism/

- Political Theology. *Language and Diversity in the Divine Intention—Genesis 11:1–9.* Retrieved from https://politicaltheology.com/language-and-diversity-in-the-divine-intention-genesis-111-9/

- Semantic Scholar. *Isaac Multiplex: Genesis 22 in a New Historical Representation.* Retrieved from https://pdfs.semanticscholar.org/55bf/ecc6e0ab37995e25b71708b24fc581c8c484.pdf

- Chabad.org. *What Does Jacob's Ladder Symbolize?* Retrieved from https://www.chabad.org/theJewishWoman/article_cdo/aid/5706938/jewish/What-Does-Jacobs-Ladder-Symbolize.htm

- Regent University. *Joseph: Authentic Leadership Forged in the Crucible.* Retrieved from https://www.regent.edu/journal/journal-of-biblical-perspectives-in-leadership/joseph-leadership-qualities

- Bible Study Tools. *Moses and the Burning Bush – Bible Story Explained.* Retrieved from https://www.biblestudytools.com/bible-stories/moses-and-the-burning-bush-bible-story.html

- Christianity.com. *What Is the Significance of Parting the Red Sea?* Retrieved from https://www.christianity.com/wiki/bible/what-is-the-significance-of-parting-the-red-sea.html

- New Brighton MC. *Manna from Heaven: A Lesson in Trust and Gratitude.* Retrieved from https://www.newbrightonmc.org/post/manna-from-heaven-a-lesson-in-trust-and-gratitude

- Study.com. *Moses & the Golden Calf – Story & Interpretations.* Retrieved from https://study.com/academy/lesson/golden-calf-story-significance-facts.html

- Vocal Media. *The Ten Commandments: The Basis of Judeo-Christian Ethics.* Retrieved from https://vocal.media/journal/the-ten-commandments-the-basis-of-judeo-christian-ethics

- The Bible Journey. *Deborah and Barak Defeat Sisera.* Retrieved from https://www.thebiblejourney.org/biblejourney2/28-the-israelites-face-continuing-opposition/deborah-and-barak-defeat-sisera/

- Studocu. *Understanding the Reduction of Gideon's Army.* Retrieved from https://www.studocu.com/en-us/messages/question/7865979/how-does-the-reduction-of-gideons-army-from-32000-to-300-men-underscore-the-theme-of-gods-power

- Coggin Church. *Judges: Strength in Weakness—Lessons from the Life of Samson.* Retrieved from https://www.cogginchurch.org/sermon/strength-in-weakness-lessons-from-the-life-of-samson-4r3nr

- Israel My Glory. *Ruth and Boaz: The Story of the Kinsman-Redeemer.* Retrieved from https://israelmyglory.org/article/ruth-and-boaz-the-story-of-the-kinsman-redeemer/

- Working Preacher. *Commentary on 1 Kings 18:17–39.* Retrieved f        r        o        m https://www.workingpreacher.org/commentaries/narrative-lectionary/elijah-at-mount-carmel-2/commentary-on-1-kings-1817-19-20-39

- Britannica. *Biblical Literature – Elisha, Prophecy, Miracles.* Retrieved from https://www.britannica.com/topic/biblical-literature/The-significance-of-Elisha

- Daily Radio Bible. *Walking in God's Light: Isaiah's Vision of Hope and Restoration.* Retrieved from https://www.dailyradiobible.com/blog/walking-in-gods-light-isaiahs-vision-of-hope-and-restoration

- Biblical Life Lessons. *Jeremiah: The Prophet of Resilience and Hope.* Retrieved from https://biblicallifelessons.com/jeremiah-the-prophet-of-resilience-and-hope/

- Bible Resources. *Education in Ancient Israel.* Retrieved from https://bibleresources.americanbible.org/resource/education-in-ancient-israel

- The Gospel Matters. *Ecclesiastes: On Life, Meaning, and Man's Ultimate Responsibility.* Retrieved from https://thegospelmatters.wordpress.com/2012/01/14/ecclesiastes-on-life-meaning-and-mans-ultimate-responsibility/

www.ingramcontent.com/pod-product-compliance
Lightning Source LLC
Chambersburg PA
CBHW061747120626
46550CB00005B/1920